The
QUESTIONS
of JESUS

Questions asked by Jesus,
Questions people asked Him.

To Kit

JohnAvery

JOHN AVERY

THE SPARKS SERIES

THE SPARKS SERIES

ISBN: 978-0-9986507-4-6 (Paperback)
ISBN: 978-0-9986507-5-3 (eBook)

Cover design by Nada Orlic
Formatting by Luca Funari

Many of the pieces in this collection first appeared on *www.BibleMaturity.com*.

CONTENTS

The
SPARKS SERIES

The pieces I write are not exactly devotionals though they have some of the flavor of a devotional: they are short enough to be read in a few minutes and can be used daily for a few weeks, each is a reflection on at least one Bible verse, and some life application is encouraged. However, the pieces are designed to stimulate deeper reflection than the average devotional. I think of them as sparks.

Jesus' life and words frequently challenged people's established ways of living. He didn't come to bless life as we know it; He invites us to lay down our old ways and receive His kingdom life instead. When a wildfire rages through brush it quickly consumes the dead and the dry. After the rain, and the space of a few weeks, new life sprouts. I pray that these pieces will be sparks to lives that are surrendered to burning and committed to the slower process of nurturing kingdom ways in place of the old.

My prayer is that a fire would ignite in your brain, fire up your thinking, race to your heart, and jump from the tips of your fingers, toes and tongue. Feed the flames so that your thoughts turn to passion, and your passion to action. May it be of such intensity that, everywhere you walk, every life that you touch is in turn set on fire.

No fire has value except the fire of the glory of God. The words of the Bible are more important than mine. For the sake of space, I have only included a few verses in each piece. So, please take time to reflect on each Scripture in its context and, if possible, read any parallel accounts. Imagine the scenes and consider the characters. As I read the passages, the Spirit's finger pointed at things in my life and inspired each piece; ask Him to work in your life too. It's His finger that beckons us out of our old ways and points us to the ways of Jesus.

May you burn with His fire as a result of reflecting on these simple sparks.

Look out for other compilations of short pieces on topics like:

- The Kingdom of God
- Our Identity as Children of God
- Conversation with God (commonly called prayer)
- Faith in God
- The Spirit of God
- Following the Voice of God (calling and guidance)
- Revival from God
- Prophets of God
- Names of God
- Followers of Jesus (what it means to be a disciple)
- Kings of Israel (David, Saul, and others)
- Fathers of Faith (Abraham, Jacob, and Moses)

Introduction to the
QUESTIONS
of JESUS

Questions. We ask them for many reasons. People did the same to Jesus. Some were simple, healthy requests for information or clarification, to learn from Him or to get guidance. But, like us, some people used them to express hurt, fear, indignation, unbelief, or anger. Enemies attempted to deflect Him, accuse Him, or trap Him with weaponized questions. Other questions were laced with the poisons of selfishness, cynicism, suspicion, and control that all reject His authority.

Jesus used questions too. He directed most of them at people's thinking. Questions helped engage His listeners when He used life sketches to make a point. Sometimes they highlighted obvious things that people were reluctant to admit. He often explored motives and the roots of injustice and other evils. He thought differently from both religious and irreligious minds; His questions exposed, challenged, and corrected both groups. They pointed to His kingdom ways.

When Jesus asked Bartimaeus, "What do you want me to do for you?" (Mark 10:51), it was as though He handed him a menu ranging from simple appetizers and side dishes to five course meals. Bartimaeus presented his legitimate physical need first. Jesus gladly met it. Jesus always receives us as we are, but He doesn't want us to stay that way. After Bartimaeus received his sight, he began following Jesus—enjoying the complete meal deal.

Jesus' conversation with a Samaritan woman (John 4:1-26) gives us another angle on what we want from Jesus. She had no idea who He really was. Jesus said if she had known Him, she would have asked for eternal life.

I assume that most people who read this book have a good idea who Jesus is. Whatever that idea is, let's allow our knowledge and faith to be stretched. As you reflect on these pieces, imagine Jesus asking you, "What do you want me to do for you?" Ask for as much of His new life as you can get; there's no limit to what He has to give.

WHERE'S JESUS?

(Context: Luke 2:41-50.)

Head counts help keep families together. Most parents do a subconscious count when they set out. Even with a largeish family squeezed into an SUV, that's straightforward. However, it was easy to lose a dusty child in a convoy of relatives, friends, and animals strung out on a rough road through the Judean hills long before cell phones.

It happened to Jesus when He was twelve years old. His parents had taken Him to Jerusalem. One day's journey towards home, they realized He was missing.[1] They returned and eventually found Him in the temple—three days later.

Most twelve-year-olds would have missed their parents after a day. Not Jesus. He was happy hanging out with the temple teachers. Mary and Joseph were hurt. Apart from the anxiety of losing Him and imagining what might have happened to Him, there was the embarrassment of admitting to everyone that they had forgotten to count their kids. Four brothers and at least two sisters are a lot, but they still fit on the fingers of two hands.[2] Once the tears of relief had subsided, there were questions.

---

1. According to custom, Mary may have traveled with women while Joseph went ahead with men. Perhaps they each assumed Jesus was with the other, without checking. However, the same ideas expressed in this piece could still apply.
2. Matthew 13:55-56 tells us about Jesus' siblings.

[Jesus'] mother said to Him, "Son, why have You treated us this way? Behold, Your father and I have been anxiously looking for You!" And He said to them, "Why is it that you were looking for Me? Did you not know that I had to be in My Father's [things³]?" (Luke 2:48-49)

In situations like this, assumptions are often the source of the tension. Parents assume the worst and think their fragile offspring are insensitive to their concerns. Kids think parents will pay attention to more changes than the growth lines scratched on the door jamb, dated, and never painted over.

Jesus was surprised they had spent three days scouring Jerusalem. Apparently, twelve-year-old Jesus saw life differently; it was obvious where He would be. His identity was already in His relationship with the Father; that was natural and the priority. Of course He would be in the temple.

But why the temple? After all, Jesus said later that the Father is not restricted to sacred spaces; He is spirit (John 4:21-24). Also, 75% of the recorded visits of Jesus to the temple or synagogues ended in conflict. So He wasn't there for the location; rather, He sought the "things" of His Father. In this case, that meant discussing Jewish Scriptures—our Old Testament— with the teachers. And He wasn't soaking up sermons. Jesus was in their midst, stunning them with His questions and answers (Luke 2:46-47). Was He learning, or were they?

Jesus never fits expectations well; He thinks and behaves differently from us. We often have a hard time figuring out where He's coming from. He longs for everyone to embrace His ways because that's what God designed us for. Still, change is hard for us; some sort of tension is inevitable. That difference is a theme throughout His life. It's the reason for most of His questions, and His answers to other people's questions. Already, as a boy in the temple, Jesus was in business with His Father—challenging and changing thinking.

Perhaps His parents should have known Him better. Anyway, it's good for us that they didn't count heads before returning home.

---

3. Forget the word 'house'; the Greek simply reads, *"en tois tou patros mou."* No houses anywhere!

The
PATERNITY TEST

(Context: Matthew 3:13-4:11. Parallel: Luke 3:21-22; 4:1-13.)

Behold, a voice from the heavens said, "This is My beloved Son, with whom I am well-pleased." Then Jesus was led up by the Spirit into the wilderness to be tempted by the devil … The tempter came and said to Him, "If you are the Son of God, command that these stones become bread." (Matthew 3:17-4:3)

It didn't begin with *who, what, when, where, how,* or *why*, or end with a question mark, but the "if" raised questions. "Are you the Son of God?" "Are you sure?" The questioner already knew the answer to the first. However, he wanted to aim straight for the jugular of Jesus' self-esteem; sow seeds of self-doubt by suggesting the second question; nip heaven's counterattack in the bud. The next temptation followed the same pattern, "Prove what a tight relationship you have with your Father, jump off the temple. He promised catchers!"

God's promises don't need preliminary trials. Doubt starts us on a quest to prove things; the quest to prove things can start us doubting. You see, by trying to prove things we have accepted that they are in question. It's a path that spirals down to a dark valley. Climbing out again is hard. Only a secure person can resist the temptation to provide immediate evidence to a taunter. Jesus was secure. He knew who He was and He knew that the devil knew.

The best advice is to do what Jesus did, stand firm against the temptation to prove oneself.

Spending time and energy proving things also distracts us from what we are supposed to be doing. To pass the wilderness test Jesus had to focus on who He was and what He was called to. The Father had spoken His affirmation and filled Him with His Spirit—no need to question or prove those things. He knew He was called to obey, even through suffering. That was His narrow path to glory. Only a confident and obedient child of God can walk it to the end. There are no shortcuts—including the one the devil suggested next (Matt. 4:8-9).

Perhaps we should view the lonely, dry, hard seasons of our lives in the way Jesus saw His. They are the very places in which we most need to absorb the truth of our adoption as God's children rather than following our instinct to muster our resources to satisfy our needs and generate a sense of meaning. Resisting temptation reinforces our identity as children of God.

BUSINESS OPPORTUNITIES

(Context: John 2:1-11.)

Occasionally, Jesus shocks us. Take His question to His mother, Mary, at the wedding in Cana. It sounds rude.

When the wine ran out, the mother of Jesus said to Him, "They have no wine." And Jesus said to her, "What business do you have with Me, woman? My hour has not yet come." (John 2:3-4)

In western cultures, one does not call one's mother, "Woman"! However, in Jesus' culture it was polite. His question, though, takes more explaining. The Greek phrase is, *Ti emoi kai soi?* It is a translation of a Hebrew idiom, *Mah li valakh?*[4] Both literally mean, "What to me and to you?" Lacking a verb, it is possible to translate it in different ways depending on the context. So, Jesus was probably asking something like, "Is it any of our business (that they have no more wine)?" Not rude, but surprisingly dismissive.

The phrase occurs in two other incidents in which demoniacs say it to Jesus:

Just then there was a man in their synagogue with an unclean spirit; and he cried out, saying, "What business do You have with us, Jesus of Nazareth? Have you come to destroy us? I know who you are: the Holy One of God!" (Mark 1:23-24; Luke 4:34)

---

4. It is found, for instance, in 2 Samuel 16:10.

15

He said, *"What business do You have with me, Jesus, Son of the Most High God? I implore you by God, do not torment me!"* (Mark 5:7. See also Matt. 8:29; Luke 8:28)

The men (or the demons that possessed them) were asking the question in an attempt to get Jesus to leave them alone. "What do we have in common?" Or, more pointedly, "We have no business together."

There are times when it is right to not interfere, probe, or insist on helping somebody. This was not one of them. Jesus was not intimidated. He did not take directions from demons. He would not be pushed away. His business was to demonstrate the power of the kingdom, and freedom for the oppressed. With simple commands and a little demonic drama, Jesus freed the men. May God give us the wisdom to know when to be gently insistent for the sake of the kingdom.

Back at the wedding, despite Jesus' apparent dismissiveness, Mary was insistent. In fact, she seemed to ignore Jesus. Instead, she rallied the servants. Jesus told them to fill the waterpots and then He performed His first sign, turning the water into wine (John 2:1-11).

Is it possible that, as He began His ministry, Jesus was hesitant, like many of us are? We will never know exactly why Jesus sounded reluctant to act. But could it be that things that seem trivial, inconvenient, irritating, intimidating, or none of our business are the very things that God arranges as opportunities for us to do kingdom business in? Kingdom business is all about turning lights on, freeing people from evil, and injecting some umph into celebrations.

Tug o' War

(Context: John 3:1-21.)

It's night. We can imagine Jesus resting under a Jerusalem arbor in the smoky orange light of oil lamps. Along comes Nicodemus, shadow-jumping to avoid recognition. He honors Jesus by calling Him a teacher from God because of His signs.

Following a brief dialogue about rebirth, Nicodemus asks, "How can these things be?" Jesus responds, "You are the teacher of Israel and yet you do not understand these things?" (John 3:9-10).

The 'things' are in the conversation that precedes the questions: Jesus says new birth is necessary to see the kingdom of God. But Nicodemus asks how birth can happen for an adult. Jesus repeats that birth of water and the Spirit is necessary for entry to the kingdom of God because only the Spirit can beget spiritual life.

Jesus' question is a beckoning challenge to Nicodemus to correct his own faulty teaching so that he can understand Jesus. The teacher of Israel, a leading spiritual guide for the nation, does not understand life in the Spirit.

Jesus ends with sad words that compare people who come to the light because they align with truth with people who hide in the dark because they deal in evil. Then Nicodemus seems to dive back into the shadows—back into his spiritual night. (Note the sad irony.)

What was going on in Nicodemus? Maybe a tug of war. Perhaps a genuine desire to know who Jesus was but a desire too weak or blind for him to die to his old life and be born to the new one. He was unable to break loose and sail like a leaf in the wind.

Later, during the trial of Jesus, Nicodemus stands up for due process (John 7:50-52). This time his colleagues snap a question at him: "You are not also from Galilee, are you?" It's a warning shot, "Whose side are you on?" "Are you with us or not?" It threatens to cut him in different directions. "If you stand up for Jesus, this is how we'll treat you: like one of those despised Galileans. We'll discredit your expertise on messianic prophecy, and trash your reputation as a Pharisee." It was a lot for Nicodemus to lose. To the end of the Gospels there is no indication that Nicodemus ever chose Jesus.

Jesus never caught Nicodemus by the sleeve to persuade him. Jesus stopped at a clear explanation and an invitation. His way is so gentle compared to the tugs from the groups we get our identity from. He sees no value in a manipulated relationship; love is only genuine when it is freely given.

We're all in a tug of war. It's important to evaluate the ties that bind us to our peers and communities. How do those ties compare to the direction and methods of Jesus? Will we choose Jesus?

Unspoken Questions

(Context: John 4:1-42.)

Sometimes our most important questions remain unasked. Perhaps we give up trying to translate feelings and thoughts into words. At other times we assume there is no one with the will or ability to respond, so why bother asking. Then there are situations when we don't even understand what is available. If only we knew, our lives might be so different. Consider the story of a woman:

Meeting the stranger was awkward. He was resting by her well; she couldn't avoid Him. Trying to focus on getting water and getting out of there, she lowered the bucket. But He ruined things; He spoke. "Give me a drink." His Galilean accent, subtly different facial features and tassels[5] showed her he was Jewish.

"How is it that you, though You are a Jew, are asking me for a drink though I am a Samaritan woman?" (For Jews do not associate with Samaritans.) Jesus replied to her, "If you knew the gift of God, and who it is who is saying to you, 'Give me a drink,' you would have asked Him, and He would have given you living water." (John 4:9-10)

---

5. Alfred Edersheim, in *The Life and Times of Jesus the Messiah*, says Jews wore white tassels while Samaritans had blue ones.

"Odd man," she probably thought. "If he's got some other water source, why doesn't he get his own drink?" It came out as, "Can you out-do Jacob, the well-digger, then?" (John 4:11-12).

The man persisted. He didn't mean well water; He meant spiritual water, an unstoppable spring of life. The woman caught a vision of indoor plumbing, but nothing more (John 4:13-15). As the conversation progressed, no names were exchanged, but she went from calling Him, "Sir," to perceiving Him to be a prophet. Then, because Samaritans believed that the only prophet to follow Moses would be the Messiah, she became open to His messiahship. Don't think that Jesus frowns on a limited understanding of His nature or that He intentionally obscures Himself. It was Jesus who steered the entire conversation to the point of confirming her speculation, "I am He, the one speaking to you." (John 4:26) He wants to be known.

Jesus is no stranger to most people reading this, but how limited is our relationship with Him and is it growing? Do we respectfully call Him, "Sir," but keep Him at a distance? Is He Master, but only selectively? And if He is Lord, what does that really mean? Impressive? Helpful in a bind? Worthy only of people a lot better than me? Jesus' human veil makes it hard to grasp the fact that He is Yahweh, God Almighty, Creator and Redeemer. Human confusion and misconceptions plague us all; the mirror is indeed dim and distorted.

Our typical prayer habit includes a shopping list. We know what we need and have good ideas about how those needs can be met. "Here you go, Jesus. How soon can You cross them off?" But isn't that doing something like the woman—limiting our expectations to our world of needs? Limiting Him! If only she had known who the strange man really was, she would not have joked about Him saving her a trek to the well. Instead, she might have asked, "Lord, will You satisfy my deepest thirsts with your living water that springs up to eternal life?" He would have done so, of course; and He will for us too—if we ask.

Let's turn the initiative back to Him. After all, He already knows what we need. Wouldn't it be better to toss the shopping list and frame our question something like this: "What do you have for me today and what new things do you want to teach me about yourself as you arrange them?" That would free Him to give us the very best and to steer the relationship between us deeper. Many people worry what He will do if they don't spend enough time with Him; the exciting question is what will He do if we include Him in every moment? The more we understand who we are talking to, the more we will surrender to the Giver and His gifts.

BIG PARTIES

(Context: Luke 5:27-32. Parallels: Matt. 9:9-13; Mark 2:13-17.)

It's hard to hide a big party in a small town with an outdoor lifestyle and no sound-proofing. The Pharisees and scribes noticed Matthew's and frowned. Then they asked a question that, of all the questions in the Gospels, is probably the best cue for explaining Jesus' mission.

"Why do you eat and drink with tax collectors and sinners?" And Jesus answered and said to them, "It is not those who are healthy who need a physician, but those who are sick. I have not come to call the righteous to repentance, but sinners." (Luke 5:30-32)

The question is an example of the clash between two worldviews. Usually, Jesus is the one exposing mindsets and motives that are contrary to the kingdom way. Here, the religious leaders take the initiative. Their question implies at least three things.

- These people are bad. Tax-gatherers were considered traitors because they helped the Romans to exploit their Jewish subjects. Identified by bad behavior, or even being the victim of a disease or disability, sinners supposedly spoiled Israel's chances of the Messiah coming. Both groups were despised.

- There is no good reason to party with them. If Jesus was really a good man He would not mix with these people. Jesus is bad.

- Of course, it also implies that the Pharisees and scribes had expert knowledge of who and what satisfies God—that they knew the difference between good and bad.

So, their title for Jesus, "Friend of Tax-Gatherers and Sinners" (Luke 7:34), was not meant to be kind. "Like arrows, the words were designed to hurt, but they unintentionally advertised the wide embrace of God. As Jesus reached out His hand to sinners, an accusing finger pointed straight at His cold-hearted, self-assured opponents."[6]

Religion[7] has a different worldview to the kingdom of God. Religion is a system often run by respected authorities. It believes qualifications are required for a relationship with God (be or do certain things and avoid other things). Religious people are quick to judge and condemn. Religion often supports or tolerates social systems, politics, and traditions that conflict with God's heart. The Pharisees and scribes wouldn't dream of compromising their beliefs and accepting Jesus' kingdom; with their complex system, they had too much at stake. Worse, they hid the key, preventing others from entering, especially the ones they despised (Matt. 23:13; Luke 11:52).

However, the spiritually and socially sick are precisely those who most need (and often know they need) the Physician. They are likeliest to accept His prescription and take His medicine. They are the poor in spirit who most easily inherit the kingdom because they have little to lose and everything to

---

6. *The Name Quest – Explore the Names of God to Grow in Faith and Get to Know Him Better*, by John Avery, Morgan James Publishing, 2015. Page 253. Used with permission.

7. Like most of my comments about religion, I use the word for a system of Christian beliefs and practices that seems to agree with biblical theology but lacks the power of a living relationship with God modeled by Jesus with His Father. But I am not the judge of who the label fits or of the final outcome of religion.

gain. Being despised they tend to avoid religious places and people. That's why Jesus made house calls and did open-air clinics.

Who are today's despised? One indicator is when people admire Jesus but think church is not for them. Another sign is whose presence in religiously inclined Christian gatherings shocks or offends the regulars. Is it the homeless, mentally challenged, or addicted? What about sex workers or LGBTQs searching for truth? The distinctions made could be about color, language, or culture, even different "Christian" practices—anything we do not easily identify with or understand, especially when, in our circles, it has a negative value. When divisive thinking mixes with our beliefs it becomes harder to accept that someone from another group could be on a legitimate quest for life.

That's not Jesus' way. In His kingdom, earthly barriers are down (Eph. 2:14). Jesus said people will be surprised who's at the big party in heaven (Luke 13:22-30).

A STUPID QUESTION?

(Context: John 5:1-9.)

For a paralytic, whose world was limited to a poolside in a bustling city, there was only one way to receive healing. His faith focused on the rippling of the pool that indicated an angelic visitation. The winner of the race to the wavy water won the prize of restored health (John 5:2-9).

Jesus walked into the competitive world of the pool and one hopeless human had his understanding of healing exploded. Jesus adopted no special posture and uttered no exceptional words, not even a profound prayer.

Jesus upon seeing the man lying there and knowing that he had already been in that condition for a long time, said to him, "Do you want to get well?" The sick man answered Him, "Sir, I have no man to put me into the pool when the water is stirred up, but while I am coming, another steps down before me." Jesus said to him, "Get up, pick up your pallet and walk." Immediately the man became well, and picked up his pallet and began to walk. (John 5:6-9)

"Do you want to get well?" Is that a stupid question? But Jesus used the question to point to a door in what seemed like an impregnable wall in the man's mind. As far as the paralytic was concerned, healing was well-nigh impossible. In his condition, winning the race to the rippling pool was unthinkable. For sure he wanted to be well, but there were a hundred reasons why it would never happen. Couldn't Jesus understand that?

Jesus' words, though, were more of an offer than a question. Healing was available in the absence of an angel. The true Healer needed no special circumstances; His ordinary words announced the arrival of health: "Arise, take up your pallet, and do what you have been unable to do for thirty-eight years—walk."

We must never allow our faith to focus on the presence or absence of conditions or special techniques. Jesus is the object of faith. Let's invite Him into our limited worlds to explode our experiences of God.

KICKING
the HABIT

(Context: John 5:1-47.)

My favorite Star Wars line was spoken by Obi-Wan Kenobi to an alien pusher who wanted to sell him death sticks: "You want to go home and rethink your life." It captures the challenge behind most of Jesus' questions.[8] To enjoy life as God intended it means progressively learning a new way of thinking. That life begins with faith in Jesus and the Father (John 5:24). However, faith doesn't always come easily.

For many Jews, their worldview blocked faith in Jesus. The main obstacles were the high value they put on their traditions, the gap between their expectations of the Messiah and Jesus' behavior, and His lack of official credentials. He had never been ordained by a respected rabbi and He flouted some of their traditional applications of the Law (not the Law itself). When Jesus healed a paralytic man by a pool on the Sabbath and told him to walk home carrying his mat, He scored two violations in one shot (John 5:8-16). Then He claimed equality with God—three! He became a wanted man (John 5:17-18).

Despite their diligent and exhaustive Scripture studies, the Jews were blind to everything that pointed to Jesus (John 5:39-47). Underlying that blindness was another problem—their back-patting pals.

---

8. 76% of Jesus' 165 questions aimed to challenge or change people's thinking about God and His kingdom and He asked 56% of them of His followers.

I have come in My Father's name, and you do not receive Me; if another comes in his own name, you will receive him. How can you believe, when you accept glory from one another and you do not seek the glory that is from the one and only God? (John 5:43-44)

Those Jews were not alone; we're all susceptible to over-valuing what others think of us. The closer our friends are, or the more valuable our association with an influencer is, the more 'glory' their affirmations give us.

Now, don't get me wrong, we need friends, we are told to encourage one another, and it's wise to seek counsel. Most of us fit somewhere in a line of authority. We are expected to do what our superiors say; we expect the same of those we are over. We should aim to satisfy our customers. However, there is a fine line between the dynamics of relationships that strengthen our life of faith and those that dampen it. Every relationship and community lies somewhere on a continuum between life-giving influence and spiritual poison.

That's what illicit drugs are—poison. "Death stick" is an apt name. And, like drugs, communities can be addictive. The Jews of John five lived in a tight group adhering to common beliefs and practices; their views bounced around the communal echo chamber. Agreement, companionship, affirmation, inclusion, recognition, respect, promotion, and authority, all had become poisonous, synthetic substitutes for 'glory,' and oh so hard to kick. What made them poisonous was that they were faith-blockers. The community united around ideas and practices contrary to Jesus.' Disagreement meant expulsion; withdrawals would be painful. Seeking glory from community blocked belief, but really it was unbelief that made the distracting and numbing effect of that kind of community so attractive. Where else can we go if we won't follow Jesus (John 6:67-68)?

Perhaps Jesus' attitude towards relationships is the hardest part of His life to grasp and to imitate. It's easy to notice that He was unflinching in the face of criticism. It's harder to admit that He didn't seem to need affirmation. Clearly, He was popular, but He withdrew when fans got too excited. Jesus sought the silent affirmation of His Father who whispered His will and eagerly watched as it unfolded around Jesus. To Jesus, 'family' meant faith-children who did the Father's will. He lived as the supreme example of sonship and, far from discarding community, He birthed true family.

What does that look like? It's individuals who listen to and obey the Lord's voice and encourage others to do the same. That's how the Son of God lived (John 5:19-20). Being children of God is where real glory lies; that's what we fell from and that's what we're being restored to (John 1:12; Rom. 3:23; 8:14-30). For all of us, to some extent, kicking the habit of harmful community is part of the process.

WHAT
Are you THINKING?

(Context: Matthew 6:19-34. Parallels: Luke 12:22-34.)

Jesus asked a lot of questions. Most of them provoke thought about deep beliefs or motives, and how those beliefs compare with truths about God and His kingdom. If we imagine Jesus asking us the same questions when we face similar circumstances it will give us a tremendous opportunity to explore and change our thinking. Here's an example of five questions in one well-known teaching.

For this reason I say to you, do not be worried about your life, as to what you will eat or what you will drink; nor for your body, as to what you will put on. **Is life not more than food, and the body more than clothing?** *Look at the birds of the sky, that they do not sow, nor reap, nor gather crops into barns, and yet your heavenly Father feeds them.* **Are you not much more important than they?** *And* **which of you by worrying can add a single day to his life's span? And why are you worried about clothing?** *Notice how the lilies of the field grow; they do not labor nor do they spin thread for cloth, yet I say to you that not even Solomon in all his glory clothed himself like one of these. But if God so clothes the grass of the field, which is alive today and tomorrow is thrown into the furnace,* **will He not much more clothe you?** *You of little faith! Do not worry then, saying, 'What are we to eat?' or 'What are we to drink?' or 'What are we to wear for clothing?' For the Gentiles eagerly seek these things; for your heavenly Father knows that you need all these* *things. But seek first His kingdom and His righteousness, and all these things will be provided to you.* (Matthew 6:25-33)

Jesus was teaching His new disciples and a crowd. He confronted a common set of anxieties—practical needs. We might include housing or the money that pays the rent or mortgage and buys our food and clothing. We could add the job that earns the paycheck.

He tells His listeners to stop worrying. Worrying about such things is something that spiritual orphans do; the children of God (birds and plants too) do not need to worry because heavenly Father provides for them. The healthiest way to live is to stop striving for life's essentials as though they are everything and they depend entirely on our brains and brawn. Instead, we should act responsibly but make the kingdom of God and His righteousness our priority.

- Each question explores our worldview. First, about life—Isn't life more than food and clothing? Without a Creator who designed us for a purpose, we might as well focus on practical needs and pleasures. The more we know the Father, the freer we are from futility as well as anxiety. And we learn what it means to be His children co-laboring with Him.

- How significant are we? Are we mere 'talking animals'? Of course not! God made us in His image. He loves His creation and arranged it in well-balanced ecosystems. Every plant, animal, and micro-organism is provided for in its niche. But humans are children of the Creator, caring for His creation and included in His plans.

- Often we think too highly of what we can do for ourselves. Worry gives us the illusion of power over our lives. Jesus confronted that lie. Anxiety adds nothing to the quality or quantity of life.

Deep down, we worry because we think we are alone and must fend for ourselves. Either God does not exist or He has no power or care to help us. That's a pagan view. It's the way we think before we know the Father—the old way of new disciples too. That's why Jesus gently calls such people, "you of little faith." It's not a damning condemnation; it's His way of alerting us to the starting line for the race of faith. His plan is for us to grow. Faith increases as we hear of the Father-heart of God, start taking trust steps, and find out just how faithful He is to care for us as we follow Jesus and seek His kingdom.

DODGY REASONS

(Context: Luke 6:46-49.)

"Now why do you call me, 'Lord, Lord,' and do not do what I say?"
(Luke 6:46)

"Sorry, I didn't catch what you said. I don't have much time to focus and there's a lot of background noise right now."

"Frankly, I don't grasp the relevance and importance of what you say to my present life or to my future."

"Let's think about which kinds of people this question most applies to. Some really need to hear this."

"It's too hard. I am not strong enough yet. Baby steps, right?"

"Stating my loyal association with you is enough for me. It comforts me to know you as a friend. Dare I say it? It satisfies my need for religion, acceptance, and assurance about the future."

"I must maintain relationships with my people; even the ones who also call you 'Lord' don't take you *that* seriously. I would alienate them."

33

"Obedience can wait; there's time. It's a sunny day; there's no flood coming."
(Luke 6:47-49)

"I have some excellent ideas that will glorify you, Lord. I am so excited to express my love in those ways, Lord. And so many powerful things are happening in our group lately; we have such a sense of your presence, Lord."

"Shush now! Enough talk. I need to work on my study of Luke 6:46. I have some great ideas for a group discussion, perhaps even a section in a book."

The
GOLDILOCKS ZONE

(Parallel: Luke 7:31-35.)

Jesus said some pretty harsh things about "this generation." Let's assume for a minute that He was talking about the people of first-century Judea. He called them evil and adulterous because they craved a sign and were unrepentant and unresponsive to Jesus (Matt. 12:41-45; Luke 17:25). He also added "unbelieving and perverted" (Matt. 17:17), and "sinful" (Mark 8:38). In a short parable, Jesus described a generation who were not happy unless they were calling the tune. Perhaps we should call them "Generation C," for control and compromise.

To what shall I compare this generation? It is like children sitting in the marketplaces, who call out to the other children, and say, "We played the flute for you, and you did not dance; we sang a song of mourning, and you did not mourn." For John came neither eating nor drinking, and they say, "He has a demon!" The Son of Man came eating and drinking, and they say, "Behold, a gluttonous man and a heavy drinker, a friend of tax collectors and sinners!" And yet wisdom is vindicated by her deeds. (Matthew 11:16-19)

Their approach to John the Baptist was like playing a jig and condemning him for not dancing. On the other hand, they wanted Jesus to plod along in time with their funeral march. This might be about staying in control by demanding that Jesus and John follow their cues. Or perhaps they wanted to maintain a religious Goldilocks zone. You know, porridge at just the right temperature.

In religious terms that means having enough passion to not be cold, but not so much passion that one stands out from the crowd. Passionate people make the crowd feel awkward because they seem apathetic in comparison. It's best to not be cold because most people think 'faith' is a good thing, but don't be so hot to get labeled 'extremist' or 'fanatic.' We all put some limit on what we will believe because we know that faith means nothing without a corresponding lifestyle. If we are following Jesus, He will keep testing and extending our limit. Religious behavior hardly changes; it's all about behaving in just the right ways to keep people comfortable—including ourselves. The Goldilocks zone is pleasantly lukewarm. Sadly, Jesus gags at lukewarmness (Rev. 3:15-16).

Were Jesus' comments limited to those alive around the same time as Him? In one passage, the generation Jesus spoke of would experience the end times, including the return of the Son of Man (Matt. 24:34). So, perhaps Jesus used the term 'generation' more broadly, to describe those in the typical human condition of sticking with the crowd.

Jesus ignored the music and the jibes. He is not in step with religious legalism; but neither does He condone sin. He's criticized by pagans for exposing sin; condemned by legalists for loving sinners. We will find Jesus when we walk His uncomfortable middle path, led by Him, not by "this generation."

DIRECTOR'S CUT

(Context: Matthew 13:1-23. Parallels: Mark 4:1-20; Luke 8:4-15.)

"The man in the boat was such fun. I loved his stories! He told them so well. What did they say his name was?"

"I forget his name, but he's great. I especially liked the one about the seeds, and the birds that gobbled most of them up. Let's find out where he's speaking next and arrive early before it gets too crowded."

Meanwhile, *"the disciples came up and said to Him, 'Why do You speak to [the crowds] in parables?' And Jesus answered them, 'To you it has been granted to know the mysteries of the kingdom of heaven, but to them it has not been granted. For whoever has, to him more shall be given, and he will have an abundance; but whoever does not have, even what he has shall be taken away from him. Therefore I speak to them in parables; because while seeing they do not see, and while hearing they do not hear, nor do they understand.'"* (Matthew 13:10-13)

Jesus had just told His famous parable of parables with its cast and props: pesky birds, vicious thorns, obstructive rocks, and mysterious seeds sown by a nameless sower. It is one of only two parables that Jesus ever explained.

Luke is the most honest. He says that the disciples approached Jesus later. "By the way, Jesus, what did your story actually mean?" Matthew hides

37

their ignorance. Regardless, Jesus explained the plot to His handpicked followers. At first, it seems unfair, even exclusive, that they should get the special edition, the Director's Cut.

But wait, parables are a heart test. Scatter a few carefully chosen words among a crowd and see what responses sprout up. Give it a few minutes and some people will have lost every word to a flock of fluttering distractions. Wait until the crowd faces the mid-week heat of their tough careers and quarrelsome families—lush resolutions will have shriveled. Within a month, life's thorny vines will have squeezed the last sap out of any remaining seedling that did not find good soil. You see, Jesus was not making a point that we should avoid seed-snatching Satan, worrisome weeds, and a rubble-strewn life—they're widespread. Even the best soil can become compacted, or spoiled by thorns and rocks. He was urging good soil maintenance—soft hearts devoted to nurturing kingdom words to produce fruit.

Jesus was not giving His apprentices a preferential explanation so they could pass a test that the crowd would fail. Even when the disciples had a cast list and knew the storyline, their response to the parable still depended on the condition of their hearts. God is the revealer of mysteries; He will gladly show us what we need when we ask. But then His words test our hearts.

Are the ears and eyes of our hearts open? Are our hearts soft and warm to the things of God and pulsing with faith? Or are they coated with the plaque of intellectualism or religious business as usual? The mysteries of the kingdom of heaven are like seeds; humble, teachable hearts are fertile soil that will bear fruit.

ANSWER
the QUESTION

(Context: Matthew 8:23-27. Parallels: Mark 4:35-41; Luke 8:22-25.)

My senior years at high school were spent writing essays. Teachers believed that the best preparation for university was learning to research a subject and condense the findings into carefully structured arguments. It worked well, except when students missed the point. Then the red ink appeared: "Answer the question!"

If the disciples had been more careful to answer Jesus' questions to them, they might have learned faster. Several times Jesus commented on their little faith: trusting the Father for practical needs (Matt. 6:30), in a storm (Matt. 8:26), sinking rather than walking on water (Matt. 14:31), forgetting to bring bread on a trip (Matt. 16:8), and failing to cast out a demon (Matt. 17:20).

When we read the Bible it can be helpful to imagine details of the scene, including the tone in which things are said. But in truth, we never know for sure any details beyond what the passage (and any parallel passages) tells us. Sometimes we assume the wrong tone and imagine facial expressions inaccurately. We do this to each other too. Phone conversations hide body language; email and text messages leave us clueless about tone too. So we read Jesus' words and perhaps imagine Him frowning and wagging a finger as He rocks in a wave-thrashed boat on Galilee.

"Why are you afraid, you men of little faith?" (Matthew 8:26)

Then we reflect on our own failures, anxiety, lack of fruit, unanswered prayers, and a track record of thousands of other examples. Shame becomes our accepted norm. We learn to live at a distance from a God who seems to stand, hands on hips, tut-tutting at our little faith. Our God puts such unrealistic expectations on us, or so it seems.

When we look closely at the incidents, Jesus always adds a question to His comments about little faith: "Don't you think that God cares more for you than He does birds and plants?" (Matt. 6:25-32); "Why did you doubt?" (Matt. 14:31); "Do you not yet understand or remember [the miracle of multiplied food]?" (Matt. 16:9-11).

Part of the process of growing in faith requires the same attention to the questions that are implied whenever we struggle to believe and trust. As we mature, we learn to ask the questions of ourselves and to hear the Spirit's gentle answers. That's what the disciples did when they failed to cast out a demon (Matt. 17:14-20). The answers always point to a different way of looking at life: ourselves as treasured and cared for children of the King; God as supremely powerful and ready to show His compassion and glory to people. Fear and unbelief evaporate in those warm truths.

So, when we recognize our little faith, let's shove shame aside. Instead, let's answer the questions that point us away from unbelief towards greater faith.

FREEZE-DRIED FRIENDS and FAMILY

(Parallel: Mark 6:1-6.)

Do you know that we freeze-dry people? What I mean is that we tend to see them as they were when we last knew them; we struggle to accept that God changes people. Our image of them is stiff and brittle. When a new reality in someone's life challenges our inflexible view, the image shatters and leaves painful, sharp fragments that can damage the relationship. Jesus experienced the phenomenon and commented on it:

He came to His hometown and *began teaching them in their synagogue, with the result that they were astonished, and said, "Where did this man acquire this wisdom and these miraculous powers? Is this not the carpenter's son? Is His mother not called Mary, and His brothers, James and Joseph and Simon and Judas? And His sisters, are they not all with us? Where then did this man acquire all these things?" And they took offense at Him. But Jesus said to them, "A prophet is not dishonored except in his hometown and in his own household." And He did not do many miracles there because of their unbelief.* (Matthew 13:54-58)

Nazareth was little more than a village.[9] From the day that Mary and Joseph returned with the infant Jesus to the time when He began His ministry, everyone knew His story. In Nazareth, His inner perfection was missed

---

9. Various sources suggest a population of 4-500.

and His everyday life probably appeared ordinary. The people of Nazareth knew nothing of His nativity in Bethlehem. His first miracle happened over the hills at a wedding in Cana. The Jesus the locals knew was a craftsman perhaps supporting His mother and six or more siblings. When Jesus began to teach and do miracles, their image of Him suddenly proved to be fragile.

Some of us know what the rejection of our new reality by loved ones is like. Perhaps they knew us when we were a wreck with legs. It hurts when they can't adapt to our new health and freedom. A healthy life with the Lord inevitably results in spiritual growth. But for anyone living at a distance, it can be hard to adjust to our increasing maturity.

Others of us, like the people of Nazareth, are guilty of the unbelief that makes no room for changed lives; the old images are more convenient. Our sin is not so much against the individual as it is against God. The challenge is to believe that God changes people—from sinners to saints and from ordinary people to spirit-filled children of God.

The lesson for those of us that are faced with a family freeze is to be humble and gracious. Our warmth can melt the old images and remold them around our new reality. We should do the work that we can among our own people, but be prepared to move on to places where there is greater openness to the new things God is doing in and through us. Sometimes God grows us by leading us to a new home where our neighbors immediately accept us for who we have become. However, ideally, if we stay current with our friends and family, they will witness the change in us and we will see them grow too.

Let's believe in the power of God to transform lives. Let's encourage one another as we mature.

A GLASS
HALF FULL

(Context: John 6:1-71.)

Some people never seem satisfied. Give them something good and, shortly afterward, they come back wanting more or better. A crowd of Jews was like that. One day they were applauding Jesus as the prophetic successor of Moses because He had multiplied a boy's lunch to feed them (John 6:14). Next day they tracked down Jesus for seconds. He urged them to work for everlasting food. So they asked,

"What are we to do, so that we may accomplish the works of God?" Jesus answered and said to them, "This is the work of God, that you believe in Him whom He has sent." So they said to Him, "What then are you doing as a sign, so that we may see, and believe you? What work are you performing? Our fathers ate the manna in the wilderness." (John 6:28-31)

Notice the irony. They had just been on the receiving end of a miracle and acknowledged Jesus as a prophet, but they asked for another sign. What was going on?

- On the surface, they wanted another free meal. Jesus knew that (John 6:26). Using spiritual-sounding language and asking for a sign was their cover for scrounging. Moses was the hero who provided daily manna; how convenient it would be if this upgraded prophet would eliminate trips to the grocery store. If this was the sum of their thoughts, they had

43

clearly ignored the implications of their own recognition of Jesus as the prophet.

- Moses was the lawgiver; wouldn't the Messiah strengthen his Laws, perhaps supplement them? So, what works should they do, Jesus? His instruction about believing in Him seemed too easy for them in their performance-based culture.

- Too easy for Him too! He needed to prove Himself properly before they would believe. Perhaps yesterday's miracle didn't qualify. If they had preconceived ideas about what signs were messianic, it appears that turning one bag lunch into a banquet for thousands wasn't one of them. Impressive, but not on the list! The glass of evidence was half empty.

- It's possible that all three reasons worked together, that their expectations and incredulity closed them off to any belief in Jesus. So, when Jesus claimed to be the living bread from heaven, they grumbled (John 6:41). "Impossible. We can't believe it, so it can't be true." They knew Him as a building contractor from Nazareth; they knew His family. And the idea of eating His flesh! Well! (John 6:52)

Some of us are hard to satisfy. Perhaps we are like those Jews—scrounging to get our earthly needs met even though Jesus promised everything to those who prioritize His kingdom. Maybe our preconceived ideas about Jesus get in the way of meeting the real Jesus more completely.

It's also common to struggle with what seems like God's patchy record. We experience answered prayers, but the excitement can wear off in the face of unanswered ones. Miracles happen, but not always. We think that perhaps the last one was a fluke or a coincidence. Shouldn't the King of kings demonstrate His sovereignty consistently? Shouldn't the glass be full?

Some people will never be satisfied with the answer to the head-scratching, but here it is: Jesus announced and launched God's kingdom; it's expanding, but not yet complete. We live between initiation and completion. Miracles and answered prayers are an expression, on earth, of the King's will.

We're promised that, if we ask according to the royal will, it will be done (1 John 5:14-15). Unanswered prayer is likely a sign that we don't understand God enough, that His will lies in another direction or time. We mustn't take unanswered prayer as fuel for skepticism; rather, take every answered prayer and miracle as examples of the kingdom breaking in a little more. The glass *is* half full, *and getting fuller.*

MASTERING LIFE

(Parallels: Mark 8:34-38; Luke 9:23-26.)

Life: We are most familiar with the gentle whoosh in our ear on the pillow every second or so, the exhilaration of scaling a ten-thousand-foot peak and seeing the magnificent view, a newborn's cries, the look in the eyes when our loved one receives our precious gift, and the reminder screamed by the void that remains when everything we possessed is nothing but a pile of smoking wreckage. Life, as we best know it, compels us to pursue pleasure and dodge destruction. If we're honest, many of our prayers follow that same compulsion.

The Master of life did it differently. Jesus spoke of two levels of life, one worth far more than the other. However, like so many of Jesus' teachings, His words sound cryptic. They are designed to probe in search of receptive hearts, just like the seeds needing good soil in His parable of parables. Here's an example:

If anyone wants to come after Me, he must deny himself, take up his cross, and follow me. For whoever wants to save his life will lose it; but whoever loses his life for My sake will find it. For what good will it do a person if he gains the whole world, but forfeits his soul? Or what will a person give in exchange for his soul? (Matthew 16:24-26)

He's not suggesting recklessness or telling us to carelessly throw life away. By all means, enjoy it, but select and arrange every part to honor Him and serve His purposes. Don't worry, that includes rest, relationships, recreation, and the occasional caramel macchiato—we need them. However, when choices come, don't try to preserve or retrieve aspects of life that are disconnected from Him. Hold things loosely (Luke 14:26, 33; 17:30-33). Allow Him to prune as much as He wants.

Our translations sometimes add to our confusion. "Life" and "soul" in the passage represent the same Greek word, *psyche*, four times. What Jesus meant was that if we try to save our life in this world we will lose our soul-life—the core of who we are—the life that is designed to continue forever. Soul life is made for an eternal relationship with God, a relationship that starts in this world—if we choose it.

Before we can make a wise choice, we must allow Jesus to scan us with His uncomfortable words and questions. What makes up our present life? To answer another of Jesus' questions, it's certainly more than food or clothing (Matt. 6:25). What would be left if everything was suddenly ripped away? How full is our heavenly treasure chest because of generous self-giving (Luke 18:22)? What residue of relationship, focused on Jesus and His kingdom, would remain? Jesus' questions recommend a cost-benefit analysis so we can discover the truth—the soul life is priceless.

Jesus was offered the world's best. He rejected it (Matt. 4:8-10). The cross He spoke of was His final choice. It was a Roman execution device. They forced rebels to carry one in a shaming parade before impaling them on it. Jesus understood the conflict between this world and His kingdom; the world sees both Master and followers as rebels. So we will have to face choices too and must be prepared to choose Him, no matter the cost. Are we prepared to live so differently that we will be mocked or shunned as fools, or taken for rebels, by some of our family, friends, and the communities and political or economic systems we live under? It might not be a literal cross, but people have plenty of ways to resist and reject whatever seems to threaten life as they know it.

APPRENTICES

(Context: Mark 9:14-29. Parallels: Matthew 17:14-21; Luke 9:37-42.)

"Teacher, I brought you my son, because he has a spirit that makes him unable to speak; and whenever it seizes him, it slams him to the ground, and he foams at the mouth and grinds his teeth and becomes stiff. And I told your disciples so that they would cast it out, but they could not do it. And He answered them and said, "O unbelieving generation, how long shall I be with you? How long shall I put up with you? Bring him to me!" ... *When He came into the house, His disciples began asking Him privately, "Why is it that we could not cast it out?" And He said to them, "This kind cannot come out by anything except prayer."* Some old manuscripts add "fasting." (Mark 9:17-19, 28-29)

Sometimes the most interesting thing is not the answer to a question but the fact that the question was even asked. For the nine disciples to wonder why they could not cast the mute spirit out of the boy shows expectation. They knew they should have been able to do it. They knew it was one goal of their apprenticeship to Jesus. They had actually done something similar on their earlier mission trip (Mark 6:13). Theirs was a very practical question, like learning to ride a bike and then falling off one day and wondering, "Whaaat? How could that happen?"

The challenge during any learning process is staying focused on the lesson's goal. It is easy, when class is out, to revert to our old ways. Perhaps the father threw them off with an expectation. It's in his words. When Jesus returned, the father said, "I brought *you* my son." Had he hoped for the specialist rather than the interns? "Hey guys. Is Pastor Jesus around?" "No, sorry. He went mountain climbing. Can we help?" It's a common attitude in our circles; people expect the "best" and we feel obliged to give them the "best." That means the expert, the one with the certificates or the charisma. If not that person, then call the team leaders. If they're up the mountain with the expert, we do our best but without confidence. Or, "Call the office on Tuesday for an appointment. He might be back; He's unpredictable." However, healings and deliverances were in their curriculum. So, after Jesus had straightened things out, the nine apprentices who had not gone climbing with Jesus asked their question.

Hearing Jesus' answer in a negative way will squish almost anyone's confidence. "It's extremely difficult." "You're not praying or fasting enough." "There's something lacking in your spiritual disciplines." Notice that none of the imagined negatives provide any pointers to help apprentices succeed. So, hear Jesus' statement positively, "This kind *can* come out, but requires prayer and fasting."

Prayer and fasting come with off-putting baggage. In short, they can sound like rigorous drills only enjoyed by toughened members of Christianity's special forces, not the average Joe disciple. We just quit before we get exhausted, as well as embarrassed. They sound like that because we have been bombarded with so much instruction about prayer (probably not much on fasting) that it can seem overwhelmingly technical and tangled. Another problem is that we tend to imagine ourselves as negotiators asking God to do things, forgetting that petitioning is only one aspect of prayer. We often lose sight of the essence of both prayer and fasting.

So, if Jesus wasn't telling His disciples they had to do dozens more spiritual squats or needed better skills of persuasion, what did He mean? Think of prayer as conversation with God and fasting as a physical expression of our hunger for Him, then the idea becomes focused. The motive is not to collect a portfolio of miracle stories; it's union with Him. But miracles will likely follow. As we demonstrate, by fasting, that we value spiritual life more than the physical, our spirits become aligned with Him. As we commune with Him, we become tuned in to His will and ways, ready to respond like Him. Viewing prayer and fasting like that makes sense of words from Paul that otherwise sound like an impossibly high standard. "Pray at all times in the Spirit." (Eph. 6:18; 1 Thess. 5:17) The Spirit of the risen Jesus never leaves on a trip; He's with us; He fills us. That makes the difference. Does anyone have a problem spending all day every day chatting and bonding with a perfect friend? "Show me what you are doing. Show me what you want me to do."

TAX SEASON, MIRACLE SEASON

Life has its ups and downs. Have you ever returned from a reinvigorating trip to find a tax demand in the waiting mail? That's how Peter must have felt when Jesus and His disciples returned from the Mount of Transfiguration. Tax collectors saw Peter coming.

"Does your teacher not pay the two-drachma tax?" He said, "Yes." And when he came into the house, Jesus spoke to him first, saying, "What do you think, Simon? From whom do the kings of the earth collect customs or poll-tax, from their sons or from strangers?" When Peter said, "From strangers," Jesus said to him, "Then the sons are exempt. However, so that we do not offend them, go to the sea and throw in a hook, and take the first fish that comes up; and when you open its mouth, you will find a stater. Take that and give it to them for you and Me." (Matthew 17:24-27)

Assuming that it ended as Jesus indicated, perhaps this was Jesus' strangest miracle. It raises questions like: What was the point? And, was it necessary? Surely Peter and Jesus could have rustled up four drachmas somehow.

Several of Jesus' other miracles seem similarly unnecessary—until we view them as demonstrations. These miracles indicate an extravagant kingdom breaking into ordinary life events—just for show! There's no need to wait for the boat to come to shore when you can walk on water. Why not bless fishing friends with record-breaking catches? Don't buy more plonk when Jesus can make fine wine from water.[10]

Miracles speed or override natural processes. Jesus seems to have watched for opportunities to do them to demonstrate the abundant power of the kingdom in everyday life. His miracles were a taste of heaven, a glimpse of the glory of human life as God intended it.

That's something to remember as we go about our daily routines. What opportunities arise to act with the authority of God's children and invite heaven to earth? In Jesus' time, sickness and poverty had few remedies. Jesus was famous for healing miracles and He fed hungry crowds. They comprised the bulk of His demonstrations of the kingdom. Modern medicine, social safety nets, and caring charities alleviate many problems. Don't despise governments or organizations for caring, but don't forget heaven's solutions either. Physical and practical needs are a chance for God to shortcut human solutions and to be glorified.

The second point—the one Jesus made—was about privilege. God's children are not subject to the world's limitations. But, although we are exempt, we humbly avoid offending. Instead, our Father, the King, protects us and provides for us. If it feels, on occasion, like a free ride ... it is.

---

10. Matt. 14:22-33; Luke 5:4-11; John 2:1-10; 21:4-6.

THUNDERSTORMS

(Context: Luke 9:51-56.)

Thunderstorms form under special conditions. High convective clouds with swirling updrafts and downdrafts cause water and ice droplets to collide. The collisions dislodge electrons and generate super-charged areas within the cloud. The energy discharges in a flash of lightning followed by a crash of thunder.

Circumstances sometimes do something analogous inside us. Faced with unclear wording in an insurance policy and an agent reluctant to press the underwriter for definitions and clarifications, I became contentious. I wasn't rude. I simply stood my ground and laid out the details of my concerns and the potential for legal problems if the policy was not clear. My brain kicked into overdrive. Thoughts raced. I spent a few hours analyzing the policy, defining words, anticipating problem scenarios. It was hard to switch off, even to sleep. In the end, it was resolved. I got a suitable policy and I felt satisfied.

Or did I?

The truth is that during my brainstorming, I felt disturbed. I wasn't impolite, pushy, or frustrated; instead, I remained calm and gentle. I wasn't wrong to ask for clarification. But something inside me was wrong. My brain was so electrified I couldn't stop it swirling about the policy details. My spirit had taken shelter in a corner, waiting for the storm to subside.

We all have special conditions that trigger us. Jesus had two followers who must have been especially prone to freak outbursts. He gave them the nickname "sons of thunder" (Mark 3:17). Once, James and John took offense on behalf of Jesus because a Samaritan village refused to host Him. The brothers wanted to firebomb the village. "Lord, do you want us to command fire to come down from heaven and consume them?"[11] Jesus pointed to the core of their problem:

"You do not know of what kind of spirit you are; for the Son of Man did not come to destroy people's lives, but to save them." (Luke 9:55) Then Jesus and His followers simply moved on.

Jesus' observation is vital. What kind of spirit are we of? The world trains us in self-confidence and self-expression with the idea that who we are is set, and we are basically good. We sometimes debate nature versus nurture, but do we ever consider that the source of who we are has a spiritual component and can change? Indeed, it would be better if it did change. The pyroclastic brothers' inclinations probably developed as they 'grew up'; Jesus offered them a new life from a new source. Jesus calls us to die to self, to be reborn and filled with the Holy Spirit, like a spiritual oil change.

Behavior and words can be measured on a scale just like thunderstorms. Some people deserve a "severe storm warning." They are manifestly evil, cruel, uncaring, dishonest, seething, irritable, manipulative, etc... Others (like me, usually) control their responses. The lightning stays in the clouds and never strikes anyone. We can be calm, polite, patient, gentle, and give wise responses. But if all those 'nice' attitudes come from the self and not the Spirit they may only boost our pride. If people are observant, they will still sense the gloom and the rumbles. Only the Holy Spirit can take us beyond refraining from harm to actually loving people and doing good that leaves a lasting blessing.

Be aware of your natural self. Don't hate or reject it, but invite the Holy Spirit to take over. Learn to walk away from conditions that stir up storms of self-life, if necessary. Let the Spirit of Jesus be your life source.

---

11. Perhaps remembering Elijah in 2 Kings 1:9-12.

MY NEIGHBOR'S NEIGHBOR

(Context: Luke 10:25-37.)

We use the word "neighbors" to mean people living right next to us or perhaps across the street (they brought us a plate of cookies when we moved in). We aspire to be good neighbors to each other (bringing a ladder and helping to prune that awkward tree). The meaning of the Greek word, *plesion*, is about the same: "the near one." Two people living near each other are neighbors to each other. Neighborliness begins with me being alert to needs around me and crossing the road, or the property line, to help.

When Jesus repeated the old command to love one's neighbor as oneself, He knew that neighborliness is a two-way street. That is clear from the way that He explained it to a lawyer who wanted to know who to target with his love.

Wanting to justify himself, he said to Jesus, "And who is my neighbor?" (Luke 10:29)

Jesus told a story about a poor Jewish guy who was almost killed by thugs, ignored by two respected religious leaders but helped by a despised Samaritan. Jesus ended with His own question.

"Which of these three do you think proved to be a neighbor to the man who fell into the robbers' hands?" And he said [avoiding the word, "Samaritan," perhaps], *"The one who showed compassion to him." Then Jesus said to him, "Go and do the same."* (Luke 10:36-37)

Follow the flow of the logic: Who proved to be a neighbor to the bandits' victim? The Samaritan, of course—the one who showed compassion. But instead of allowing the lawyer to answer his own question by reflecting on all the kind people who had helped him, and thinking about how he could return a little love to them, Jesus told him to go and *do the same*. Find a needy person and help them out. Take responsibility for their need. Care for them at your own expense. If the lawyer really thought he could justify himself by loving a neighbor, Jesus had just shown how unattainable self-justification is.

Their conversation had begun when the lawyer asked one of the most important life questions, "What shall I do to inherit eternal life?" The Law provided an outline but no clear definition. It was easy to keep the letter of the Law and still miss the lifestyle that the Law pointed to. The Law said, "love your neighbor," but left a cozy loophole. People cherry-picked the easiest people to love, and relationships went just like the rest of the world's. That's why Jesus had to stress how different the kingdom life is. Love should go far beyond the nice people who help us and include even our enemies.

If you love those who love you, what reward have you? Do not even the tax-gatherers do the same? And if you greet your brothers only, what do you do more than others? Do not even the Gentiles do the same? (Matthew 5:43-48)

BEYOND CARING

(Context: Mark 4:35-41; Luke 10:38-42. Parallels: Matt. 8:23-27; Luke 8:22-25.)

Okay, I admit it. On the day that I wrote this, I was angry with God. I had been excited at all the things He had been doing, but then it seemed that everything was blocked or diverted. All my prayer and faithfulness seemed to go to waste. Why didn't God intervene to keep the vision on course? We could have been half way to revival by then. Didn't He care that it could all be lost?

"Didn't He care?" The words echoed back at me. They reminded me of two occasions when Jesus' followers said the same thing:

[Jesus] was in the stern, asleep on the cushion; and they woke Him and said to Him, "Teacher, do you not care that we are perishing?" (Mark 4:38)

[Mary] was seated at the Lord's feet, and was listening to His word. But Martha was distracted with all her preparations; and she came up to Him and said, "Lord, do you not care that my sister has left me to do the serving by myself? Then tell her to help me." (Luke 10:39-40)

In each case, Jesus seems ignorant or unconcerned about apparently pressing issues. We can imagine the disciples shaking Jesus awake with frightened and frustrated voices. "Grab a bucket and bail!" Martha probably burst through the kitchen door flapping her apron, somewhere between tears and a temper tantrum.

However, when we look closely, Jesus took caring to a new level. In the storm, Jesus' simple word calmed the cause of everyone's anxiety and revealed His authority and glory. Paddling hard or sloshing out the excess water would have won Him a slap on the back like any other responsible buddy. But by stubbornly refusing to behave as we would like Him to, He introduces us to heaven. That's His way of working. Later, He walked, unflinching, to the cross because He knew resurrection followed it. We want our lives and visions to be plain sailing; He prefers miracles. Of course He cares about storms—but He goes beyond our ideas of caring.

Jesus did not seem to care much at all about Martha's concerns. Instead, He put them in context. To rest in the presence of the Lord is the priority; all the worries of everyday life are unnecessary compared to that. Mary had it right.

It takes a lot to tear ourselves away from our plans and core concerns and focus on responding to life the way Jesus taught us. Laying down our instinct to arrange life "just so" is hard. Wanting to avoid storms and suffering is natural, but not always God's way. It's right to alert Jesus to turmoil and injustices, but don't expect Him to deal with them the way you want Him to. Our anger at God is a sign that we need to trust Him at a new level or allow Him to rearrange our priorities.

TRUE SERVICE

It's risky being entertained in someone else's home when you need to talk. Unless you have considerable clarity, tact, and strength of character, the host will tend to limit or control the meeting. Did you come with important, perhaps delicate, things to discuss? How awkward will it be to say them while the hostess draws attention to her latest and greatest cheesecake? Isn't it more polite to go with the flow? After all, it is their house. Jesus faced a situation like that.

Martha welcomed Him into her home. And she had a sister called Mary, who was also seated at the Lord's feet, and was listening to His word. But Martha was distracted with all her preparations; and she came up to Him and said, "Lord, do You not care that my sister has left me to do the serving myself? Then tell her to help me." But the Lord answered and said to her, "Martha, Martha, you are worried and distracted by many things; but only one thing is necessary; for Mary has chosen the good part, which shall not be taken away from her." (Luke 10:38-42)

Martha's question, "Do you not care?" reveals her assumptions. Martha, like most of us, was thoroughly absorbed in her way of living—and hosting. It never occurred to her that her hospitality goals were anything but correct. For Jesus to just sit and chat seemed uncaring. As the hostess, Martha expected support from her sister, Mary. Based on that thinking, she tried to recruit Jesus to instruct Mary to help meet those goals. "He should take care of me; that's part of His job."

Most of us would gently nod towards Mary, "You know, perhaps you should go help. We'll talk more later, if there's time." Jesus does life differently. He acknowledged Martha's many concerns but He pointed to Mary's better choice—listening. It wasn't that Jesus didn't care; rather, Martha cared too much about her serving.

We have no idea what Jesus was saying to Mary. That's not the point. We need to notice her surrender to His lordship. Mary seems quite familiar with Jesus' feet (John 11:32). Later, she slopped so much expensive perfume on His head that it dribbled and dripped to His feet (Mark 14:3-8; John 12:3). To the frugal, it seems wasteful. To frenetic Martha, she seems passive, even lazy. Martha's concept of serving missed something.

True service begins with listening to the one we are serving. (Do they even like cheesecake?) Only when we know a person's wishes can we begin to serve. And we mustn't run off too quickly as soon as we hear the first part of the instruction. The objective may sound simple but the way we accomplish it must reflect the character of the master too. Do we understand His timing? How should we respond to resistance? True service requires lots of careful listening. True servants stay really close to the feet of the master. True servants care more about knowing Him than about any task He might assign.

It's risky, Jesus, when someone opens the door of their life to your knock. There are different kinds of host. Some want to impress you with their skillful service. Many hand you a "To Do" list. Only a few know you as the supreme interior designer who will rearrange things to the best effect. Everyone gets to choose what they allow you to do after they have opened the door. After all, it is their life.

LIVE BAIT

(Context: John 8:1-11.)

When I want to catch rats under a house, I use smelly cheese to get their attention so that they grab it and spring the trap. The Pharisees wanted to trap Jesus. They dragged live bait, kicking and squealing perhaps, right under his nose.

The scribes and the Pharisees brought a woman caught in the act of adultery, and after placing her in the center of the courtyard, they said to Him, "Teacher, this woman has been caught in the very act of committing adultery. Now in the Law, Moses commanded us to stone such women; what then do You say?" Now they were saying this to test Him, so that they might have grounds for accusing Him. But Jesus stooped down and with His finger wrote on the ground. When they persisted in asking Him, He straightened up and said to them, "He who is without sin among you, let him be the first to throw a stone at her." And again He stooped down and wrote on the ground. Now when they heard this, they began leaving, one by one, beginning with the older ones, and He was left alone, and the woman where she was, in the center of the courtyard. And straightening up, Jesus said to her, "Woman, where are they? Did no one condemn you?" She said, "No one, Lord." And Jesus said, "I do not condemn you, either. Go. From now on do not sin any longer." (John 8:3-11)

Jesus oozed with mercy and the Pharisees knew it. Their victim had no hope of living unless Jesus intervened. She had been caught red-handed violating the seventh commandment; the penalty was clear and justified. In their eyes, Jewish religious Law prescribed the solution for sin—death by stoning would wipe the stain from among God's people. "What do you say, Jesus?" Would Jesus respect the religious system and apply it to the woman or would He be unable to resist His insatiable appetite to extend mercy to sinners? If He reached out in mercy the legal bar of the trap would snap down and crush Him along with that odious adulterer.

The Pharisees stood back smirking and watched as their rat sniffed at the trap. He scratched a little in the dust and then looked up. With a few select words, he exposed their danger.

The trap, so cleverly set for Jesus, was bigger than the Pharisees knew. If they relied on the Law to do its job they would never escape its reach or its force. The wisest or the most guilt conscious among the Pharisees began to blend with the crowd and shuffle away, mumbling. Soon, even the youngest, most zealous and idealistic Pharisees were gone. Only the sinner remained. Jesus had done what He so skillfully does; He had turned the trap on its makers. They were so absorbed in their religion that they refused to accept Jesus as God's solution to sin, bettering the Law. When Jesus confronted their guilt, pride propelled them back to their religious holes. Only a wretched woman had the humility to stick around to receive the guilt-free life that Jesus alone could give.

This incident shows there is no contest between law and grace in Jesus' mind; instead, the two work together. Unlike the Pharisees, Jesus knew the true role of the Law. In the absence of Jesus, the Law has the authority to throw stones at sinners; in the presence of Jesus, the Law bows to His authority. The Law exposes our sin, highlights our need for cleansing, and points to our Savior.

We have our own religious systems, don't you know? Does yours pretend to be the best solution for sin? The test of any system is whether it puts Jesus in the center and allows Him to deal with sin and dole out life. What then do *you* say?

BELIEVING *in* FULFILLMENT

(Context: John 8:12-59.)

One of the ironies of prophecy is that, when it comes to pass, there are people who refuse to believe its fulfillment. Sometimes we construct a warm and comfortable nest of expectations around a prophetic hope without realizing that those ideas have become more precious than the object of hope itself. Fulfillment requires the dismantling of what was intended as temporary prophetic scaffolding. Some people object to that dismantling. That was the case when Jesus fulfilled messianic prophecies.

The conflict between Jesus and the Jewish religious leaders intensified during a Feast of Tabernacles. Jesus angered them when He healed a man on the Sabbath, declared that He was the light of the world, and claimed God as His Father. He also confronted their unbelief. Finally, Jesus said that if anyone obeyed Him, that person would never die.

The Jews said to [Jesus], "Now we know that You have a demon. Abraham died, and the prophets as well; and yet You say, 'If anyone follows My word, he will never taste of death.' You are not greater than our father Abraham, who died, are you? The prophets died too; whom do You make Yourself out to be?" (John 8:52-53)

The conversation was going downhill fast. That happens when people are entrenched in what they already believe. The Jews responded with a common strategy. When Jesus confronted their spiritual deafness, they discredited Him by labeling Him a demonized Samaritan, criticizing Him to deflect His criticism (John 8:47-48).

Jesus answered their scoffing questions with a thinly veiled claim to divinity. "Abraham rejoiced to see my day." And, "Before Abraham was born, I am." (John 8:54-59) Jewish writings suggest that, during his vision in Genesis 15, Abraham had peered into the Messiah's time. In His answer, Jesus had grabbed the Jews' treasured prophetic charts, thrown them down in front of them, and pointed: "Here's where we are on the map. Look at the landmarks!" The Jews considered it unbelievable effrontery.

On a previous occasion, Jesus had confronted Jewish unbelief in reference to His message and His wisdom. The Queen of Sheba had recognized King Solomon's wisdom; the wisdom of the Son of Man was greater. The people of Nineveh had repented at the message of Jonah; Jesus' words were far more important. Yet few people were ready to accept that Jesus was greater than Jonah and Solomon.[12]

Only a despised Samaritan woman had been able to frame her objection in a searching question, "You are not greater than our founding father, are you?" Jesus' unspoken but resounding answer was "Yes." Later she reached out with more faith, "Could this be the Messiah?"[13]

As God's Messiah, Jesus is greater than any of our heroes, traditions, or homemade expectations. So we should ask ourselves whether we cherish them more than Him. And, when it comes to longstanding personal prayers, promises, or words of prophecy, are we ready to live in the new world that comes with their fulfillment?

---

12. Matthew 12:41-42.
13. John 4:10-14, 25, 29.

DISLOCATION

(Context: John 9:1-41.)

One of the most painful experiences is being kicked out of a group. Relationships matter. We need the encouragement of others. We thrive on shared visions, values, experiences, and simple things like food and fun. However, it is not unusual for followers of Jesus to face the pain of separation or dislocation. It happened to a blind man once.

Jesus had just healed the man and it triggered an awkward moment—two worlds collided. The man was an odd part of the Jewish religious establishment, a synagogue member along with his parents. The system had rules and standards—quite comfortable ones if you accepted them. Sabbath was a day for rest and worship. To break that Law was a sin. Hundreds of things were on the sin list, including healing someone. Sinners could not possibly be in good standing with God, let alone speak and act with His authority. The religious leaders confidently taught Scripture *and* their opinions of what God wanted. Most people nodded in agreement. That included the blind man, who had been taught that his congenital blindness was damning evidence of sin in him or his parents.

That damned condition supported an oddly comfortable, ordered life—until Jesus passed by. Jesus ignored the restrictive Sabbath rule about not healing people. He dismissed the lie that blindness signaled sin. He shrugged off religious indignation. His world—or rather, kingdom—was different.

The miracle placed the family in a predicament. The blind man's parents shied away from admitting their knowledge about the miracle because they knew they would be kicked out of the synagogue. His relational world was woven into the religious order too, but the man could never escape the truth of his healing. All the objections of the religious leaders were stupidly irrelevant to him; he knew one thing, "I was blind, now I see" (John 9:25).

Later, *they answered him, "You were born entirely in sins, and yet you are teaching us?" So they put him out. Jesus heard that they had put him out, and upon finding him, He said, "Do you believe in the Son of Man?" He answered by saying, "And who is He, Sir, that I may believe in Him?" Jesus said to him, "You have both seen Him, and He is the one who is talking with you." And he said, "I believe, Lord." And he worshipped Him.* (John 9:34-38)

It happens in a thousand ways. The reality of God calls us away from the uncomfortable comforts of our established worlds. Our networks of relationships are stickiest. We rarely choose to leave, but tight communities react to members who start to think and act differently. The circle tightens more, the embraces exclude us, and backs are turned. Dislocation hurts.

Jesus provides a new family. It's not united by human rules and rulers but through focusing on Him. One thing begins the relationship: belief in Jesus as the Son of Man, with all that implies. Ideally, every newcomer will continue relating to their old network, explaining the changes, sharing the freedom and joy, and attracting others to the kingdom of Jesus. Sadly, rejection is common. But the new life in a new family is worth it.

Switching Labels

(Context: Matthew 12:22-37. Parallels: Mark 3:22-30; Luke 11:14-23; 12:10.)

Beware misleading labels and wicked labelers. In *The Three Musketeers*, Alexandre Dumas has a scene in which the evil Milady attempts to kill D'Artagnan by sending him bottles of wine spiked with poison. The label says they are Anjou wine but when Brisemont, the servant, samples some, he collapses and expires, writhing in agony.

Religious leaders fired barrages of labels at Jesus, attacking Him to take attention away from what He so spectacularly did. When He forgave and healed a paralytic, they shouted, "Blasphemy!" on the grounds that only God can forgive sins. Jesus responded, "Why are you thinking evil (or reasoning) in your hearts?" (Matt. 9:3-4; Mark 2:7-8; Luke 5:21-22). Then He confirmed His authority by telling the man to get up and walk home, stretcher under arm.

One winter day, some Jews almost stoned Him. He asked, "I showed you many good works from the Father; for which of them are you stoning me?" The Jews answered Him, "We are not stoning You for a good work, but for blasphemy; and because You, being a man, make Yourself out to be God." (John 10:32-33) "We don't accept your label."

A few months later, Jesus' trial concluded with the same accusation of blasphemy when He applied messianic titles and Daniel 7:13 to Himself (Matt. 26:63-66; Mark 14:61-64; John 19:7).

When it came to exorcism, their logic disintegrated. Jesus delivered a dumb blind man and people questioned, "This man cannot be the Son of David, can He?" But when the Pharisees heard this, they said, "This man casts out demons only by Beelzebul the ruler of the demons." (Matthew 12:23-24) Jesus shot back questions to give three, simple, logical rebuttals. It made more sense to recognize that Jesus' power exceeds Satan's than to accuse Him of friendly fire, but only a few people thought logically (John 10:21). Jesus continued,

Every sin and blasphemy shall be forgiven people, but blasphemy against the Spirit shall not be forgiven. And whoever speaks a word against the Son of Man, it shall be forgiven him; but whoever speaks against the Holy Spirit, it shall not be forgiven him. (Matthew 12:31-32)

Everyone agreed that, from the time of Moses, blasphemy meant misrepresenting God by putting Him down or by raising something or someone else up as equal to or better than Him. In the conflict between Jesus and the religious leaders, the accusation flew both ways: They saw Jesus promoting Himself as God, but their unwillingness to accept Him profoundly undervalued Him. Jesus did not condemn them for denying His divinity. But He said that slandering the Holy Spirit, when His works are unmistakably good, is another matter. The religious leaders were committing the unforgivable sin—switching labels. When good and evil are deliberately confused or reversed it indicates a hardness that makes forgiveness impossible because conviction cannot penetrate to bring repentance. No one accepts the work of the Spirit if they label Him 'poison.' Eventually, the labeler drinks from the wrong bottle—and poisons himself.

All this raises the question, who has the authority to label good and evil? The religious leaders based their claim to that authority on succession. For generations, priests, scribes, and teachers had studied Scripture, taught their students, and later, passed their authority on to them. Jesus claimed authority directly from His Father and pointed to witnesses: John the Baptist, His miracles, and Scripture (John 5:31-47). He also understood that trees are known by their fruit (Matt. 12:33, 35).

Some fruit takes a while to ripen. Jesus was so secure in who He was that He endured their blasphemous accusations, the sham trial, and the crucifixion. He knew His fruit was spectacular and would endure; it spoke for itself. Final vindication and evidence of the accuracy of His labels came in the resurrection and the outpouring of the Holy Spirit.

The
SIGN *of* JONAH

(Context: Matthew 12:38-42. See also Matt. 16:1-4; Luke 11:16, 29-32.)

> *Then some of the scribes and Pharisees said to Him, "Teacher, we want to see a sign from you." But He answered and said to them, "An evil and adulterous generation craves a sign; and so no sign shall be given to it except the sign of Jonah the prophet." (Matthew 12:38-39)*

The Gospels are full of signs that Jesus did. So why, when people requested a sign, did He refuse to give one except for the mysterious "sign of Jonah"? What was that sign and why was it the only one He offered?

The pattern of Jesus' responses to the questions of different types of people is part of the answer. When His disciples asked Him to explain the parable of parables or other things, He readily did so. If they asked for guidance, He gave it. Judas wondered why Jesus would disclose so much to them and not to the world. Jesus' answer was that His followers did what He asked; they didn't waste His words (John 14:22-24).

On the other hand, those who resisted Jesus often got little or no answer. False accusers and King Herod (who hoped for a miracle show) were basically ignored. The trick questions of religious leaders only received answers that exposed their mistaken worldview and their evil intentions. It was hardened people, like them, who asked for signs.

"Don't throw your pearls before swine." That seemed to be Jesus' practice. True disciples hear and obey; if anyone is unreceptive, move on (Matt. 7:6; Luke 10:10-11). That's a caution to us: what is the purpose of our questions to God? Do we want truth from Him or are we skeptically resisting Him? If resistant people had witnessed a special sign, they would probably have dismissed it just as they dismissed all the other signs and teachings. Even so, Jesus said they would get one sign. That sign, the sign of Jonah, was not a concession to cynics; it was Jesus' central act. It would function as a sign, but it had a bigger purpose.

"For just as Jonah was in the stomach of the sea monster for three days and three nights, so will the Son of Man be in the heart of the earth for three days and three nights. The men of Nineveh will stand up with this generation at the judgment, and will condemn it because they repented at the preaching of Jonah; and behold, something greater than Jonah is here." (Matthew 12:40-41)

When Jonah arrived in Nineveh, the people surely heard his amazing story. No one had ever survived swallowing by a sea monster before. Perhaps this helped them respond to his warning by repenting. Jesus knew His vindication would come after three days in the tomb. If anything could amaze and convict them, resurrection could. But it wouldn't convince everyone (Luke 16:31).

All of Jesus' brief answers to requests for signs allude to His resurrection. They demanded one when He overturned traders' tables in the temple. His answer: "Destroy this temple, and in three days I will raise it up." (John 2:13-22) Immediately after feeding five thousand people, the Jews wanted another sign (John 6:30). He spoke of being the bread of life, and about His death, resurrection, and ascension. Resurrection was the only sign He promised. Open hearts respond; hard hearts still shrug it off.

My Jesus

(Context: Luke 12:13-21.)

Once in a while, someone jumps to a conclusion about who we are before they really know us. It creates all kinds of awkwardness. Based on their impression of us, they develop expectations. We feel under pressure; they feel frustrated when we don't deliver. It was the story of Jesus' life. Here's an example.

Someone in the crowd said to Him, "Teacher, tell my brother to divide the family inheritance with me." But He said to him, "You there—who appointed Me a judge or arbitrator over the two of you?" (Luke 12:13-14)

Jesus was crystal clear about who He was and what He came to do. He had no need to try to please anyone except His heavenly Father. So, instead of allowing the awkward situation to develop (as I tend to), Jesus answered the man with a question, followed by a warning illustrated with a parable (Luke 12:15-21). The question: "Who appointed Me a judge or arbitrator?" The answer is, of course, that the man wanted Jesus to take that role. He had seen and heard so much about the wise miracle worker that he thought, just maybe, here was someone who could persuade his brother to split the inheritance more favorably.

Appointing Jesus to satisfy our personal desires is a danger that we must all be alert to. He is not "my Jesus" in the sense that He does my bidding. Now certainly, Jesus does care for us. He meets our deepest needs, provides for us, heals, guides, and so on. But there is a subtle yet vital distinction between indulging us and nurturing us into spiritual maturity. We must be honest, what do we ask our Jesus to do for us?

Following Jesus starts with bowing to Him as Lord; the walk continues with learning the will and ways of our new Lord. More and more, we have to stop demanding what we want, what we think is best, and quietly receive His better blessings. It's a whole new life. Our deepest needs are met as we surrender to His will and to this new way of living.

Two levels of life! It was a novel idea to the man, and to the crowd. On this earth, negotiating a better deal on an inheritance seems natural. Living off a surplus, like the rich farmer in the parable, is a sign of success. But Jesus warned that it's a form of greed. A higher life happens in a relationship with the heavenly Father. That relationship grows as we learn to share His values. One of those values is generosity towards the needy. Jesus immediately went on to explain that more to His disciples (Luke 12:22-34): When we care for the needy, we store up treasure in heaven. When we seek God's kingdom, He ensures a steady supply for our practical needs. Perhaps the man in the crowd was still listening. Perhaps we are too.

GOD'S UMBRELLA

(Context: Luke 13:1-9.)

It happens after almost every natural disaster. Someone suggests that God ordained it as a consequence or punishment of some sinful behavior. It has been going on for millennia. Once, Jesus got dragged into the debate.

There were some present who reported to Him about the Galileans whose blood Pilate had mixed with their sacrifices. And Jesus responded and said to them, "Do you think that these Galileans were worse sinners than all the other Galileans just because they have suffered this fate? No, I tell you, but unless you repent, you will all likewise perish." (Luke 13:1-3)

Jesus continues by adding to Pilate's atrocity a natural disaster—a tower in Jerusalem that had collapsed and killed eighteen people (Luke 13:4-5). He asks the same question, "Do you think … ?" It seems that people were speculating that the victims of both incidents somehow had it coming to them. They were sinners or debtors, singled out for justice delivered by acts of God and man.

Jesus answers again with an emphatic "No!" and a warning that the same kind of fate will come unless people repent. Then He tells a parable in which a fig tree is given one last chance to bear fruit (Luke 13:6-9). The tree is a picture of the Jewish nation, the very people listening to Jesus.

It's easy to join the crowd speculating as to why bad things happen. It's tempting to take the path that religious Jews often took—assuming that sickness and suffering were a result of sin. Not only does this thinking put terrible condemnation on unfortunate people, but it also helps us compare favorably with them and gives us a sense of assurance that we must be doing fine. Jesus says that is a false sense of assurance. If we think like that we are not aligned with God. Human abuses and natural catastrophes are not orchestrated by God. His heart is to give people (like the fig tree) not just one last chance but another chance, and perhaps another, and so on.

Repentance somehow lifts us out of this world in which we are pawns to the powers, subjects of chance, destined to become statistics. Repentance spares us from perishing at random or at the whim of a tyrant. It makes us subjects of God and brings us under His umbrella-like covering. It does not guarantee we will live happily ever after, but it does free us from the anxiety of helplessness and sets us firmly within the mainstream of the purposes and timing of a loving Father.

Whose Choice?

(Context: Luke 13:22-30. See also Matt. 7:13-14.)

Someone said to Him, "Lord, are there just a few who are being saved?"
And He said to them, "Strive to enter through the narrow door; for
many, I tell you, will seek to enter and will not be able." (Luke 13:23-24)

Why the question? There is little to go on in the context. Perhaps this person had been keeping track of responses. For sure, big crowds hung around Jesus, but He didn't heal everyone, had no influential endorsers, and His disciple band stayed small. Did the questioner want a number or just confirmation of a suspicion? Was this a cynic or someone angry that there wasn't a more conventional way into God's favor? Perhaps he or she was an amateur theologian approaching the question from the angle of personal choice versus predestination or election. Are souls pre-selected, elected, then collected? How much does it depend on God's will who 'gets saved'?

Jesus certainly did not go in that direction, but He did imply the answer. Many will search but not be able to enter; it follows that few will succeed. He pointed to a door that is possible to find but difficult to enter. It wasn't the head of the house who made the decision; it was the people who failed to find and enter the door while it was open. Proximity to Jesus doesn't count; knowing Him and being known by Him do. Unfortunately, there are easier ways and wider doors that distract us. Getting through that narrow door is one of the few things we are told to strive for.

Jesus challenged ideas about "salvation" too when He portrayed it as participation in a meal in the kingdom of God (Luke 13:29). All the expectations about Abraham's heavenly family reunion will be shattered. People will come from the ends of the earth; life's honors lists will be scrambled. Those who thought they were heirs will find themselves disinherited, while the least and the last take their places (Luke 13:25-30).

The
BIRD HOUSE

(Context: Luke 14:25-33.)

One of the most helpful workshops I ever attended began with a bird house. A consultant for a multinational oil company visited our humble missions base and donated thousands of dollars' worth of training over two intensive days.

If you want to build a bird house, begin at the end—draw a picture of what the completed bird house will look like. Then work backward. Diagram the steps you must take to assemble the house. What parts will you need? What tools? Only when you have a clear vision, a plan, and have done a little shopping are you ready for construction.

If you want to build a discipleship movement, you must be completely focused on the goal. That was Jesus' point, except that He spoke of building a tower and winning a battle:

For which one of you, when he wants to build a tower, does not first sit down and calculate the cost, to see if he has enough to complete it? Otherwise, when he has laid a foundation and is not able to finish, all who are watching it will begin to ridicule him, saying, "This person began to build and was not able to finish." Or what king, when he sets out to meet another king in battle, will not first sit down and consider whether he is strong enough with ten thousand men to face the one coming against him with twenty thousand? Otherwise, while the other is still far away, he sends a delegation and requests terms of peace. So then, none of you can be My disciple who does not give up all his own possessions. (Luke 14:28-33)

Building contractors and warrior kings are not known to take on projects until they are fully prepared. Jesus was not suggesting that we should quit because of unpreparedness but that we must do the planning and preparation.

The tower Jesus mentioned was probably a vineyard watchtower. Foundations without superstructure would be worthless to a watchman; he could never see over the vines to spot any pests or thieves. Imagine the concealed sniggers as the foolish vineyard owner passed by.

So, what is the end product of discipleship? Obviously, it is more disciples of Jesus. We are to teach them to live His lifestyle—including making still more disciples. Those disciples in turn are to make more disciples until the ends of the earth are reached. The completed picture is something like a vat of frothy brewers' yeast—vibrant and expanding. But it is about more than numbers and multiplication; a wholesome community lifestyle develops too when we are responding to Jesus' leading.

Notice that I have not used the word "church." Unfortunately, that word comes with centuries of baggage. Although the church described in the New Testament fits the picture, in some cases our church activities and organizational plans seem to distract us from Jesus' plan. We think discipleship is something churches do; in fact, disciple-making results in church. Sometimes we engage in temporary token disciple-making activities, rather than being sensitive to opportunities throughout the week. Perhaps we jump from one ministry or project to another, like rides in a fair, instead of developing relationships and gifts to the full. Are you part of a church that looks like a discipleship movement?

Let's begin with the end in mind. Let's pray and plan to start a discipleship movement, a network of disciples, growing in the Lord and making more disciples. Follow the plan. Get equipped with a few simple tools. Stay focused. But let's do it.

WAITING
for ANSWERS

(Context: Luke 18:1-8.)

How a certain judge ever got his job, I have no idea. For sure, no one gave accurate character references about him. He was supposed to give justice to people, but he was unjust. His nature was contrary to his position. Along comes a widow, close to the bottom of the social pecking order, looking for judgment against her legal opponent. The judge dithers. Nothing in him is inclined to help her.

Thankfully, it's a story (Luke 18:1-5). Jesus devised this awkward scenario of a person least likely to obtain justice seeking it from the judge least likely to give it. Only the woman's persistence caused the judge to give what he had no inclination to give. Jesus' point: If a man like that eventually dispenses justice, how much more will God, whose nature is just, give it—and quickly? It's not a parable likening God to the unjust judge but contrasting them. He used a common Jewish argument[14] from a lesser example (the judge) to a greater (God). If A is true, then B must be even more true.

> *Will not God bring about justice for His elect who cry out to Him day*
> *and night, and will He delay long over them? I tell you that He will*

---

14. Known as *qal v'khomer*, light and heavy.

bring about justice for them quickly. However, when the Son of Man comes, will He find faith on earth? (Luke 18:7-8)

Don't make the mistake of thinking the parable is about persistence resulting in answers; it is, rather, about persisting *because* God's just nature guarantees vindication and it's worth the wait. Jesus' purpose was to encourage His followers to pray and not fade, on the basis of that guarantee. Jesus' questions could be rephrased: Will we stay focused on His absolutely just nature so that our faith remains?

He had good reason to ask. Waiting with no sign of a result is a tough and frequent test. God answers some prayers, but not others. He heals some people, but not others. There are wrongs that God will right in our lifetimes; some must remain unresolved until the Son of Man returns on the day of justice. Delay is never a sign of a fault in our Judge; we can still trust Him for eventual vindication. Nonetheless, His reasons for delaying are beyond us, and the unpredictable pattern of divine intervention is a potential source of confusion, cynicism, and even unbelief for many of us. And that's the purpose of Jesus' parable and the aim of His questions: is our faith properly founded so that it will endure any amount of waiting? Enduring faith rests on something more than God's answers. It is not based on our persistence or anything else in us; it is based on the just and righteous nature of God. Such faith motivates us to remain in a position and posture to receive from God rather than moving away or failing to reach out.

WARMER

(Context: Luke 18:18-27. Parallels: Matt. 19:16-26; Mark 10:17-27.)

Growing up, we had a good-sized garden with lots of shrubs. We would play a game there in which one person hid an object and the others would try to find it. The winner got a prize. Perhaps the hidden object was wedged under the fence or placed in an old blackbird's nest or partly obscured by fallen leaves under the rhododendron hedge. Whenever one of the searching children came near to the hiding place the person who hid it might hint that they were "getting warm," "warmer," or even, "really hot." Without that clue, finding the object was difficult; the clue kept the game moving and everyone stayed interested because of the reward.

> *A ruler questioned Him, saying, "Good teacher, what shall I do to inherit eternal life?" But Jesus said to him, "Why do you call me good? No one is good except God alone."* (Luke 18:18-19)

For Jesus to zoom in on the ruler's use of an everyday word may seem picky. Wasn't the man using it respectfully to honor Jesus? Perhaps. But Jesus tends to probe heart motives, not to condemn us but to urge and invite us to what our hearts crave—eternal life. However, He plays by His rules, not ours. His question, "Why do you call me good?"[15] exposes a logical disconnect.

The deep implication of calling Jesus good is that He should be treated like God. If He is good, why was the man not following Him, obeying Him? Instead, he seems to treat Jesus like someone with helpful insights giving a TED talk —a good *teacher*. In theory, the ruler was happy to add one more item to his repertoire of admirable behaviors. In practice, his life was inseparable from his assets. He went back to that life—an unmet longing in his heart and Jesus' invitation taped to the refrigerator door of his memory.

Humans seem to have a high tolerance for that kind of disconnect. Inside we live in search mode; on the outside, we prefer our own solutions or distractions, even though listening to the hints and finding the treasure would be much more fun. In how many ways do we honor Jesus and adopt *part* of His teaching, because we admire Him, but fail to assess just how good He really is and the fuller implications for us?

Elsewhere, Jesus defined eternal life as a relationship with Him (John 17:3). If the man had fully understood Jesus' goodness, he would have realized that eternal life means closeness to Jesus. It's impossible to live the life without the relationship; it's impossible to have a thriving relationship without embracing the lifestyle of God. Perhaps the man was "getting warmer" with his Law-abiding lifestyle (though we mustn't think that the ten commandments are anything more than a skeletal expression of life with God); He just needed to cut loose from what possessed him and follow Jesus. That can only happen when we realize how precious life with Jesus is compared to anything in this life.

God knows that entering eternal life is a process only completed in heaven and that, on earth, it may wax and wane. Like the hider in the game, He does not condemn us during our search. He gives us clues to encourage us. If we want to experience eternal life more fully—to keep getting "warmer"—contemplating exactly who Jesus is really helps.

---

15. To be fair, Matthew has a different question, "Why are you asking me about what is good?" (Matt. 19:17).

COST-BENEFIT ANALYSIS

(Context: Matthew 19:16-30. Parallels: Mark 10:17-31; Luke 18:18-30.)

Peter and the others had heard the conversation between Jesus and the rich ruler who had asked what the requirements were for eternal life. Jesus had told the man to liquidate his possessions, invest in heaven by giving to the poor, and then follow Him. That set Peter doing a simple cost-benefit analysis.

Behold, we have left everything and followed you; what then will there be for us? (Matthew 19:27)

"What's in it for me?" It's a common question. Perhaps Peter had never bothered to think much about the longer-term benefits beyond his fascination with Jesus. He and his friends had left jobs, homes, and families to follow Jesus. They qualified, right? And, if Jesus had already sketched out some benefits, perhaps it was time to get details about the rewards—eternal life and the kingdom of God (Matt. 19:16, 24). Hence the rather self-interested question.

Between them, Matthew, Mark, and Luke lay out the package. Jesus promised seats of authority, eternal life, and also hundredfold returns on what they had sacrificed, even in this life (Mark 10:30). A spectacular return on their investment.

However, Mark seems to spoil things; He includes Jesus' sobering addition—persecutions. Apparently, followers of Jesus must expect to pay future costly installments. The ruler had thought his down payment of keeping the commandments would be sufficient, but his heart had to be pried from the clutches of mammon. If Peter thought that leaving and following were enough, he was missing something important.

Following Jesus was more than a walking tour of Israel. Certainly they sacrificed, "on account of My name" (Matt. 19:29). But Jesus had also called them for the sake of the kingdom of God (Luke 18:29) and the good news (Mark 10:29). That good news was about the King and His kingdom; the three are inseparable.

So far, it had been fairly easy to follow Jesus. He was an entertaining teacher with tons of practical wisdom. Although religious leaders warned against Him, it was fun seeing them humiliated by His clever responses. However, it soon became clear that Jesus was serious about His kingdom. Conflict would intensify. Every human inclination and every institution based on those inclinations eventually pushes back against kingdom ways. For the ruler, it was materialism, perhaps pleasure-seeking. For others, it could be pride, control, individual freedom, and many more. None will readily bow to Jesus—hence persecution in all its subtle and sadistic forms. But the King and His kingdom are such good news that the benefits will always outweigh the cost. No question.

FOCUSED FAITH

(Context: Mark 10:46-52. Parallels: Matt. 20:29-34; Luke 18:35-43.)

Replying to [Bartimaeus], Jesus said, "What do you want Me to do for you?" And the man who was blind said to Him, "Rabboni, I want to regain my sight!" And Jesus said to him, "Go; your faith has made you well." And immediately he regained his sight and began following Him on the road. (Mark 10:51-52)

Jesus' question to Bartimaeus, the blind beggar of Jericho, seems unnecessary. Why ask a blind person, "What do you want me to do for you?" But isn't it the question that Jesus asks all of us? It's a question that tests the focus and resolve of our faith—that's what He is looking for.

Bartimaeus demonstrated focused faith in four ways:

- When He heard that the commotion was in response to Jesus the Nazarene, he cried out. He had high expectations of the mercy of the Son of David. No one could deter him. Lies about being an unworthy, second-class citizen did not stick. He persisted.

- On learning that Jesus was calling for him, he threw off his cloak, jumped up, and elbowed his way through the crowd to Jesus. He refused to allow even his legitimate limitations to be an excuse for remaining in his condition.

- Bartimaeus boldly responded with the obvious, "I want my sight back." He believed that Jesus had the will and the means to restore his sight. He could have pointed to his other need. "Let me win the lottery so that I never have to beg again." What about other partial solutions to blindness and poverty? Bartimaeus might have chosen a better cane, a helper to lead him around and guard the begging bowl, or an all-expenses-paid home. All sensible and useful—but short-sighted.

- His was no quick fix to enhance life in his roadside niche. Everything changed for Bartimaeus. Jesus became his focus. He followed Him.

How do we respond to Jesus' open question to us? When we bring our requests to Him, do we boldly seek His highest will for us or do we assume that a partial solution is more likely? Jesus always calls to us from beyond the range of our natural sight and hearing. He has the capacity and desire to give us the very best. But perhaps we are blind to that truth. Do we feel unworthy? Maybe we are too polite to ask for the best portion. Sometimes we are only looking for a quick blessing to improve our present condition—like the comfort of a cushion for the hard ground from which we beg.

Focused faith propels us up and away from our established discomfort to follow Jesus into increasingly abundant life.

A Hiking Tip

(Context: John 11:1-44.)

I always pack a flashlight because sometimes I misjudge how long a hike will take. Once, the sun set six miles from the trail's end. I did a two-hour night hike through trees, barely able to distinguish the path from the forest floor. If the battery had failed, I would have had no choice but to bivouac, eat my last granola bar, and wait for dawn. The experience reminds me of a lesson Jesus taught.

Jerusalem Jews had tried to seize Jesus, so He had taken the disciples across the Jordan river. Then word had come that Lazarus was sick in Bethany on the outskirts of Jerusalem. Jesus did nothing for two days. His sudden announcement elicited a startled and anxious question.

[Jesus] *said to the disciples, "Let's go to Judea again." The disciples said to Him, "Rabbi, the Jews were just now seeking to stone you, and yet you are going there again?" Jesus replied, "Are there not twelve hours in the day? If anyone walks during the day, he does not stumble, because he sees the light of this world. But if anyone walks during the night, he stumbles, because the light is not in him."* (John 11:7-10)

Jesus' response was a question to engage minds and teach the importance of walking in the light. Light is a big theme in John. In many contexts it refers to the will and ways of God. Jesus called Himself the Light of the World, meaning that His presence provides light for us. People either desire more truth and welcome the light, or they prefer their old ways and reject light (John 3:19-21).

Like us, the disciples were still learning. Human nature avoids danger whenever possible. They dreaded Jerusalem; it was a death trap (John 11:16). Jesus saw things differently. For Him, danger did not exist in the light of the will of God, only on a spiritual night hike, because there is no light in us. If we stay with Him, in His will and timing, we are safe because He protects us so we can accomplish His will. Presumptuous or well-intentioned things done contrary to God's will are risky. Claiming that we are acting in faith makes no difference, that's more like magic thinking than true faith.

So, should people who think they cannot hear God or know His will feel afraid to venture out spiritually? No! God is gracious. We have a reassurance that He judges according to how much we know of His will (Luke 12:47-48). He also wants us to grow in hearing His voice and obeying—to grow in faith. If we are pursuing His presence, Jesus will lead us out of the dark into the dawn of His light—just as He led His first disciples.

The PILFERER PRETENDS

(Context: John 12:1-8.)

The scent was exquisite but almost overwhelming. The occasional, cool evening breeze through the open shutters was quite a relief. Whatever Mary had slathered on Jesus' feet was clearly top-of-the-line perfume. "Probably cost her a fortune," thought Judas. "What a waste!" (Matt. 26:8) Unable to stifle his feelings any longer, he blurted out,

"Why was this perfume not sold for three hundred denarii and the proceeds given to poor people?" Now he said this, not because he cared about the poor, but because he was a thief, and as he kept the money box, he used to steal from what was put into it. (John 12:5-6)

Judas polished his question to a shine. He phrased it carefully to conceal a dark motive while sounding bright and compassionate. Many of the questions people (including us) ask of Jesus need to be dissected and scanned to discover the deeper question. What Judas meant was, "Why wasn't it sold, and the proceeds put into the money box that I carry so that there is more for me to siphon off for myself?"

If we are honest, we probably hide wrong motives behind pure ones sometimes. It's part of human nature to have more than one reason to do things. We will probably never escape from mixed motives, even in what we do for the Lord. So I have no complete remedy, just things to watch for to avoid becoming like Judas, the pilferer.

- The cry, "What a waste!" is a warning sign—time to investigate our motives. I have invested myself in relationships by listening, loving, serving, and forgiving, only to find that the friendship was not the two-way street that I had thought it was. Worse, perhaps the person turned on me, rejecting me and all I had done. Eventually, I realize that I wasn't content to love for the sake of the friend or for Jesus; I wanted a lasting companion for myself. Similar scenarios happen when ministries fail and investments seem wasted.

- We must be completely honest with ourselves—it's part of humility. What are the selfish motives that may be drawing us to a particular activity? Is there an ulterior motive for joining the worship band—a lead with the lead, or to get on base with the bronzed bass player? When I run the youth group, am I hoping for recognition or a path to a staff position? Once we know our motives, we can make better choices. We should ask the Holy Spirit to convict us too; He often waits for an invitation. Notice that Jesus did not confront Judas; He went along with Judas' pretense about boosting charitable donations.

- At other times the Spirit does disturb us. Perhaps the personal outcome that I envisage is more precious to me than He is. That's serious pilfering, if you think about it; it grieves and distances Him. Secondary motives are usually fine until they hijack us so that we no longer follow the Lord's leading. If that happens to me, God withholds anointing and allows me to become frustrated. It's time to search my heart and re-submit to Him.

The danger with even normal, healthy motives that take over but are never satisfied is cancerous frustration. It spreads, and it spawns resentful behavior or secret self-indulgence. Perhaps Judas' frustration with Jesus' failure to tackle and topple the Romans led him to start pilfering. "After all my sacrifices, I deserve a little reward." We can get so obsessed with our selfish goals that we stop caring about His calling. So be careful, pilfering can even lead to betrayal.

Avoiding *the* Hamster Wheel

(Context: Matthew 21:23-32. Parallels: Mark 11:27-33; Luke 20:1-8.)

Circular arguments are illogical. People get irritated when someone seems to use one. The religious leaders thought Jesus was doing exactly that when He said things like, "My teaching is not My own, but His who sent Me." (John 7:16; 12:49) We can almost hear them jeering, "That's what you say." To them, He seemed to be authorizing Himself. They ignored Jesus' attesting signs, so their irritation persisted.

Why did they ignore the signs? Simply because they were frantically racing around their own hamster wheel of bad logic. It had begun well: God revealed Himself to Israel when He delivered them from Egypt. He manifested Himself on Mount Sinai and established Moses as the law-giving leader. Fast forward through priests and Scribes to a system of delegated authority. Teachers taught disciples and authorized them as the next generation of teachers. As time went on, each generation supplemented Scripture with a little more commentary, tradition, and opinion. The result was a series of rabbinical schools of teaching, a self-authorizing system with less connection to God's word. Who a rabbi's authority came from became the key issue. If you weren't running in the wheel, you weren't valid. John the Baptist and Jesus were suspect. Hence the question that followed when Jesus cleared the temple of merchants.

"By what authority are you doing these things, and who gave you this authority?" But Jesus responded and said to them, *"I will also ask you one*

question, which, if you tell me, I will also tell you by what authority I do these things. The baptism of John was from what source, from heaven or from men?" (Matthew 21:23-25)

His was a loaded question. He already knew what they believed and He knew they could not answer comfortably either way. The truth about John's source was exactly parallel to the answer about Jesus. If John and Jesus spoke for God they should be listened to. From the start, the crowds had noticed Jesus' new teaching with authority (Mark 1:22-27). The leaders did not want to anger them by denying His divine inspiration, so they refused to answer Him. He reciprocated.

Jesus wasn't dodging an unspoken accusation of self-authorization. Neither did He make circular arguments. He often stated that He was sent by God; mostly, He let miracles and wisdom speak for themselves. Resurrection was His ultimate validation. When the assessors of authenticity no longer function properly, the process must revert to more basic assessment principles in order to avoid the hamster wheel. Fruit and Scripture, rather than its interpretations, are what really matter.

They should matter to leaders too. The main arguments for a system that authorizes its own teachers and leaders are to preserve doctrinal purity and protect sheep from wolves. However, it can get out of hand as it had with the Jewish religious leaders. Control can be used to preserve personal influence, promote particular ideas, and gag others. Will people's inquiries about which church you go to or what your doctrinal beliefs are lead to meaningful relationships between followers, or are they more likely to provide excuses for rejection and division?

How should authority work in the church? Leaders should equip sheep to shepherd others, not hold them back. When leaders train people to be disciple-makers surrendered to the Holy Spirit and to each other, then those leaders have far fewer wolves to worry about. If we're in authority, we must devote ourselves to knowing God and aim to never act differently from Him. We should promote people who do the same. If we're under authority, let's never get so lazy that we stop looking beyond our leaders to the will and ways of the Father.

PUSHED BUTTONS

(Context: Matthew 21:33-46. Parallels: Mark 12:1-12; Luke 20:1-19.)

People don't like being challenged. Unknowingly, I pushed buttons once. An acquaintance posted a slanderous and inaccurate comment about a public figure on social media. I simply asked for sources, but it ignited a firestorm of abusive dismissals of me and any position that my question seemed to imply.

When Jesus entered the temple complex, the religious leaders asked a simple question. What authority did He have? Jesus handled it beautifully. Instead of dodging their challenge, or exploding, He turned their trick question back on them and they were silent (Matt. 21:23-27).

Then He told a parable about two sons whose father asked them to work in his vineyard. One said, "I will, sir," but never followed through. The other refused but later realized he was wrong and went to work. Jesus did what good teachers often do; He engaged His listeners with a question. "Which of the two did the will of his father?" The son who changed and set to work, of course. But the question did more than engage them; it had awkward implications: Tax-gatherers and harlots were putting the religious leaders to shame; they had believed John the Baptist while the leaders stubbornly refused to change (Matt. 21:28-32).

Next, Jesus told a parable about a landowner who rented out his vineyard. The tenants rebelled against the owner's slaves and then killed his son. Again Jesus engaged the leaders with another question with a clear answer,

"When the owner of the vineyard comes, what will he do to those vine-growers?" They said to Him, "He will bring those wretches to a wretched end and lease the vineyard to other vine-growers, who will pay him the fruit in the proper seasons." Jesus said to them, "Did you never read in the Scriptures, 'A stone which the builders rejected, this has become the chief cornerstone; this came about from the Lord, and it is marvelous in our eyes'? Therefore I say to you, the kingdom of God will be taken away from you and given to a people producing its fruit." (Matthew 21:40-43)

Jesus had used the questions to expose the religious leaders' rejection of the kingdom of God. Then He had predicted their destruction. His method of asking questions with obvious answers put the hearers in the uncomfortable position of having to silently back down or change.

Further, He had asked what seems like an insulting question, "Did you never read [Psalm 118:22]?" Of course they had read it; they probably had it memorized! The implication is that the words had entered brains through eyes, although the real meaning had never sunk into hearts. Jesus was accusing them of missing the point—they were rejecting Him.[16] Again, the leaders had little choice, either change their position or save face somehow. Well, they were offended and sought to seize Him when the crowds dispersed (Matt. 21:45-46). After a few more failed attempts to trap Him, the leaders gave up (Matt. 22:46).

Jesus knew that people hate to be challenged and exposed, so why did He pursue the conflict? Did He go too far? Before answering, consider three unknowns:

- The Gospels are relatively expressionless. The best we have are Greek records of a Hebrew or Aramaic dialogue—no tone of voice, no facial expressions, few other non-verbal clues. Jesus might have been smiling, playfully chuckling, or even hugging them while He exposed them. Was

---

16. Six times Jesus asked religious leaders something like "Have you never/not read ... ?" Four of those times are claims that He was the Messiah fulfilling the Scriptures (Matt. 12:3-5; 19:3-6; 21:16; 22:31 and the parallels).

He weeping as He warned them? He probably showed respect somehow. Any of those could have softened His impact.

- We have no idea whether Jesus had an ongoing relationship with the elders. He certainly saw the chief priests a few times. He ate with Pharisees sometimes. Relationships can soften disagreement.

- These men were expert legal debaters; verbal wrestling was their sport. They knew the rules and the stakes. And Jesus knew too. Even as a boy He had seen them in action in the temple. Some people are used to challenges like this. Most of the people we know are not.

We should reflect on these three things to minimize offense in our communications. As we do that, the message is more likely to be heard. But in the end, we have to accept that Jesus did offend. Within the week, He was arrested and killed. You see, Jesus knew that His worldview—the coming of a kingdom lovingly ruled by His Father—was incompatible with the religious leaders' worldview. He knew how unbending they were. He knew where the clash would eventually lead. Time was short. He gave them one last chance to change—even if it pushed buttons.

BAD ACTORS

(Context: Mark 12:13-17. Parallels: Matt. 22:15-22; Luke 20:20-26.)

Tension was building. Jesus had frustrated the religious leaders' attempt to silence Him for being uncredentialed. He had pushed their buttons by portraying them in a parable as villains and mocking their Scripture knowledge. He always seemed to have fans around Him, making it impossible to grab Him. The drama intensified.

Behind the scenes, the Pharisees gathered a few of Herod's supporters and some of their own disciples, explained their plot, and coached their lines:

"Teacher, we know that you are truthful and do not care what anyone thinks; for you are not partial to anyone, but you teach the way of God in truth. Is it permissible to pay a poll-tax to Caesar, or not? Are we to pay, or not pay?" But He, knowing their hypocrisy, said to them, "Why are you testing me? Bring me a denarius to look at." (Mark 12:14-15)

In Greece, actors were called hypocrites. They wore costumes and masks to play their parts. That was innocent pretense, but the word became negative when deceptive people used the same tactic. Luke exposes them best; they were spies pretending to be righteous to catch Him. Jesus saw through their trickery (Luke 20:20).

He also guessed why they were testing Him—they wanted to trap Him. It was a crude and ineffective snare. To tax, or not to tax, that was their question. It's common to hear people use that same simplistic 'logic,' assuming either one thing or the other is right. Call it black or white thinking, or binary reasoning, if you like. Either way you lose, Jesus. You're a Jewish traitor if you support the Imperial Revenue Service and rebellious if you don't. Jesus saw the issue colored and shaded. In His eyes, there was no conflict between paying taxes that supported Rome (though He would have called for fairness) and honoring God. His kingdom went beyond Israel and the Roman empire anyway. We make a similar mistake to the Pharisees if we think the world is more contrary to kingdom ways than it really is.

But why test Him? Why not just confront Him frankly? "Jesus, you are misleading people, destabilizing this nation. We're coming after you." They tested Him because they hoped He would trip Himself. If they could set Him up to alienate His supporters with a viral blasphemy or treasonable tweet that would place all the guilt on Him. Sometimes we do things like that. We prefer to exit confrontations blameless, so we try to shift fault to the other person. It helps keep the dirt off those nice masks and costumes, if one happens to wear them.

DEFINING LOVE

(Context: Matthew 22:34-40. Parallels: Mark 12:28-34.)

*"Teacher, which is the greatest commandment in the Law?" And
[Jesus] said to [the lawyer], "'You shall love the Lord your God with
all your heart, and with all your soul, and with all your mind.' This is
the great and foremost commandment. The second is like it, 'You shall
love your neighbor as yourself.'"* (Matthew 22:36-39)

It was easy for the lawyer to agree with Jesus' answer (Mark 12:32-34), but
love begs to be defined.

How many times have you heard First Corinthians chapter 13 used at
weddings? It is the go-to love passage, describing love in sixteen ways. But
is it a thorough definition of love or just a partial description? I suggest it is
not the whole picture. Each statement in it is true, but we can only understand love by looking at the heart of God revealed in Jesus and throughout
the Bible. If we run away with our own ideas of love, we quickly lose sight of
the King of love; we can't force our definitions on Him. His love is different.

The world has established a confusing, fallen equilibrium around
"love"—even the Christian world. We tend to muddle it with *liking* people.
Weddings bloom with romantic love. Then there's the idea of tolerance.
So long as we avoid the most obvious sins and abuses, we can accept little weaknesses, can't we? After all, doesn't First Corinthians say, "love is

patient, love is kind … does not take into account a wrong … endures all things."? You are free to do your peccadilloes so long as I am free to enjoy my peccadilloes. To "love" me, you must agree to that small print. You are even free to become more like Jesus, but don't challenge me or, well, I might have to crucify you.

Surely love does better than the popular versions that depend so much on a measure of agreement. I would suggest that healthy love focuses on what's best for the other person. Love's context is always a relationship, even a brief one; two people come closest to knowing each other's best through dialogue. That's not to say that we know the best for them; only God really knows. But here's a better definition:

Love is seeking the best for a person with the understanding that the best is always found in a relationship with God.

Love often gets frustrated. Not everyone trusts us. The sixteen points of First Corinthians are foundations for love; practicing them builds trust and smooths relationships. But, even if people trust us, not everyone wants God's way. And love never forces the best on anyone.

The definition also applies to loving ourselves. What is best for us is found in our relationship with God. We are alert to some obstacles. Sin and self-abuse obviously distance us from God. What about the cloud of unknown future factors whose influence could be healthy or unhealthy? That is where we need to live Jesus' way, "Your Father knows what you need before you ask Him" (Matt. 6:8). Instead of blindly grabbing for what some-how seems best, we should surrender to the Lord and invite Him to give His best. Sadly, God's love often gets frustrated too.

The definition of love works for God loving us and for us loving our-selves and other people, but not for us loving God. He does not need our help and cannot improve anyway. Instead, we show our love for Him by obe-dience. Jesus said, "If you love me, you will keep My commandments" (John 14:15). Complete obedience requires heart, soul, and mind; it indicates that we give Him the highest place and trust Him. That allows God's desire for our best (His love for us) to bear fruit. Our receiving His love and becoming what He intended delights Him. We love Him by accepting His love for us.

Jesus modeled love for God. He gently refused to follow the world's way. He lived in childlike dependency on the Father. Because He embraced what the Father was doing as the best for Him, "God highly exalted Him, and bestowed on Him the name which is above every name." (Phil. 2:9)

CHEAP WORDS

(Context: John 16:1-33)

Jesus is like a wise engineer. He understands that even when a material appears to be strong, that does not mean it can be relied upon; more information is needed first. During a long discourse that He gave, His disciples' understanding seemed to grow clearer and their faith stronger, but was it strong enough?

Finally, they said, *"Now we know that you know all things, and that you have no need for anyone to question you; this is why we believe that you came forth from God." Jesus replied to them, "Do you now believe? Behold, an hour is coming, and has already come, for you to be scattered, each to his own home, and to leave me alone; and yet I am not alone, because the Father is with me."* (John 16:30-32)

Peter had made a similarly bold statement earlier that evening. He asked, *"Lord, where are You going?" Jesus answered, "Where I am going, you cannot follow me now, but you will follow later." Peter said to Him, "Lord, why can I not follow You right now? I will lay down my life for You." Jesus replied, "Will you lay down your life for Me? Truly, truly, I say to you, a rooster will not crow until you deny Me three times."* (John 13:36-38)

A polite answer to such commitments might sound something like this: "Guys, I really appreciate that. Thanks." However, Jesus never seemed to do 'polite'. Politeness has a valued place in society because it preserves people's feelings and honor, but it can have a price—it sometimes veils truth. Often it is better to know the truth. So, Jesus' questions weren't tactless or cynical. He was being realistic—which means the disciples were not!

Let's put ourselves in the disciples' sandals and consider why we make bold statements that later prove to have been cheap. Here are some possible reasons:

- We get carried away by our emotions. Jesus' after-dinner speech was inspiring. He had just talked at length about the love that bound them all together and the Spirit Helper that He would send. He had predicted the future, proving His knowledge and control. Things were not only clearer; they sounded exciting. Who wouldn't jump on board more fully? However, later, when the future arrived and appeared disastrous, trust in the speech-giver vanished faster than the favorite Passover dishes had.

- We don't understand the implications of what we claim to believe. Faith in anything affects behavior in some way. Perhaps the price of action is too high, or we fail to count the cost before blurting out our commitment. Jesus discouraged that; He was up front with His follow-ers. Several times, He explained that, ultimately, they had to take up a cross—be treated as rebels to some degree or other.

- Bold claims impress audiences and satisfy real or imagined peer pressure.

- We might be out of step with the will of God, like the disciples were. It was not their time to suffer and die courageously for their faith; it was Jesus' time alone. Scripture had to be fulfilled. Their time would come later.

Jesus has no need for answers to His own questions, "Do you ... ?" "Will you ... ?" He already knows human nature. The questions were meant to sink into His followers' minds—including ours! He is not discouraging us from stepping out boldly, but first, He wants us to exercise realism like Him. We need to think like spiritual engineers considering which materials to use in a project—look at the results of stress tests. Faith is proved in the same way. Then, if a beam is not quite adequate for its job there are ways to reinforce it. The same is true with faith. With humility, we can ask for the reinforcing presence of the Helper.

It's likely that the disciples remembered Jesus' 'impolite' questions after they had scattered and denied Him. The memory probably helped them to process their failures and get all the help they could from the Holy Spirit when He came at Pentecost. That way, they went from being men of words to being men of action.

PRAYERS
of PREPARATION

(Context: Mark 14:32-42. Parallels: Matt. 26:36-46; Luke 22:39-46.)

My prayer discipline has always been fairly strong, but I have expectations. When those expectations don't get met, I lose interest. I want answers, results: feelings of His presence, peace, clarity, breakthrough in ministry, changes in the lives and ministries of others. You see, my prayers are quite transactional, even selfish. The pattern causes a problem. When I'm in a dull routine, have limited interactions with people, or face an uncertain future, prayer is difficult because results seem less likely. Trying to squeeze the same results from my plodding discipline frustrates me. Such situations require a new kind of prayer. The disciples had an opportunity to learn it.

Thursday was a strange day. The Passover meal was simple but good, although Jesus had continued His gloomy predictions about betrayal and death. Now they were in the olive grove and Jesus was more troubled than they had ever seen Him. He had asked them to watch—for what? It was hard to stay awake in the dark with a full stomach.

[Jesus] came and found them sleeping, and said to Peter, "Simon, are you asleep? Could you not keep watch for one hour? Keep watching and praying, so that you will not come into temptation; the spirit is willing, but the flesh is weak." (Mark 14:37-38)

The disciples faced an unclear future. Jesus seemed different, even distant—fewer miracles, more serious teaching. Was he running out of juice? It was hard to get motivated to pray; normal prayers didn't fit. The only topic Jesus gave them—resisting temptation—made little sense in an empty grove. However, it made sense to Jesus. When looming storm clouds veil the future, human nature tries to sidestep the threatening clouds—find an easier way. Spirits, otherwise willing to pursue kingdom ways, succumb to the temptations thrown at weak flesh. Frightening crises, a distant-seeming God, even boredom, all tempt us to resort to the self-centered coping mechanisms we learned and practiced over a lifetime. Even an uncertain future can discourage us from praying. Napping is one alternative.

What if the disciples had prayed as Jesus said? Perhaps Peter would not have drawn his sword and slashed an ear. Perhaps he would have accepted the consequences of owning his friendship with Jesus. Would the disciples have scattered, hidden, and found it so hard to believe Jesus' resurrection? Who knows what God could have done with temptation-proofed men?

Okay, I know what you are saying. "Jesus' death was necessary. This was not the disciples' time." That's true. Jesus' immediate future was a chasm that He had to cross alone; on the far side was glory, resurrection life. But could it be that the disciples were being offered something analogous? Are we?

There's another aspect to praying to resist temptation: praying for preparation. Preparation prayers aren't shopping lists of petitions. They go beyond the definition of prayer as conversation with God. Prayers of preparation in a crisis or for an uncertain future are mostly silent communion with God. We can whisper invitations and a welcoming of God to do what He wants; words of surrender, faith, and adoration; an echo of the prayer of Jesus, "Not My will but Yours." Prayers of preparation involve an expectant attitude that God is forging something magnificent beyond the gloomy horizon. He's readying us to receive it—to live an expanded experience of His kingdom. The hope and faith that accompany such prayer inoculate us against unseen temptation.

Such prayer does not purchase the increased presence of God; it is preparation for that presence. Payment without quick results is frustrating; preparation holds exciting promise. Prayers of preparation change the balance of power *inside* us. The spirit grows stronger relative to the flesh, ready for more spirit life.

FLASHPOINT

(Context: Matthew 26:47-56. Parallels: Mark 14:43-52; Luke 22:47-53; John 18:1-11.)

If we allow them to, life's awkward or threatening situations will spur our spiritual growth. They face us with our wrong thinking, which gives us an opportunity to change. Here's an example where, instead, Peter[17] reached his flashpoint while Jesus remained at peace.

One of those who were with Jesus reached and drew his sword and struck the slave of the high priest and cut off his ear. Then Jesus said to him, "Put your sword back into its place; for all those who take up the sword will perish by the sword. Or do you think that I cannot appeal to My Father, and He will at once put at my disposal more than twelve legions of angels? How then would the Scriptures be fulfilled, which say that it must happen this way?" (Matthew 26:51-54)

It took perhaps two or three minutes to unfold—an ominous mob stirred to a frenzy and barging through the trees, the betrayal kiss, the rush to grab Jesus. Peter had no time to think properly; instead, a pulse of adrenalin went to work. Peter was deeply threatened. He had invested years of his life in Jesus. His hope for a better future was in Jesus. And now Jesus was in a religious arm-lock about to be bound and led away. No one else had stepped in to defend Jesus. Peter must act.

---

17. John 18:10 names him.

Peter did what many of us do when we feel cornered—he lashed out. No one uses swords these days. Our actions, words, or looks are sharp enough. Some people are skilled at hiding their verbal swordplay behind soft, controlled tones. They win respect for that! People obstructing them hardly know what happened. Soft or sharp, our words and actions seem to do the trick, turning the intimidation back on our opponent. Usually they fail to truly free us. Often they spill life-blood and mutilate our relationships.

There in the turmoil, Jesus did what He does so well. He asked a question that faced Peter with his wrong thinking. "Is God in control, or not?" You see, if Peter had really understood the power of God, his thoughts would have moved faster than his adrenalin. He would have responded as Jesus did—calmly. Jesus knew the power of God. He understood why that power was restrained for a time. He saw how His arrest fitted into the plan of God spelled out in Scripture. God is not only powerful; He is in control. So don't fight back.

That Jesus healed a severed ear was wonderful, but frustrating to his followers. He did nothing about the main threat and injustice; He let the current sweep Him away. But that selective intervention was a signal to hell that Jesus was in control and would later conquer what was temporarily winning. It takes great faith to accept token displays of God's power.

As we walk through life trying to follow the Lord in His purposes, we will sometimes feel cornered. What we expected God to do does not progress smoothly. Finances, health, disagreements with others, lack of time, closed doors—so many ominous obstacles boast that they have the final say. But each time we feel cornered is a point where we can receive a flash of revelation. It's the opportunity to adopt new thinking about the power and control of God. Sometimes we are meant to exercise godly authority over the enemy and drive away the opposition. At other times He will lead us to a different kind of victory.

CRYING FOUL

(Context: John 18:19-23.)

Here's part of a rough transcript of Jesus' trial. The high priest had questioned Him about His followers and His teaching. He answered:

"I have spoken openly to the world; I always taught in synagogues and in the temple area, where all the Jews congregate; and I said nothing in secret. Why are you asking me? Ask those who have heard what I spoke to them; Look: these people know what I said." But when He had said this, one of the officers, who was standing nearby, struck Jesus, saying, "Is that the way You answer the high priest?" Jesus answered him, "If I have spoken wrongly, testify of the wrong; but if rightly, why do you strike me?" (John 18:20-23)

Jesus' second question probed the motivation behind the blow. We will never know whether the officer responded well or defiantly. Did he ignore Jesus? Did he back off in shame, or apologize? John recorded no answer, but we can still use the question for our reflection.

Which side of the question are you and I on? Are we the ones being interrogated and perhaps slapped and therefore in a position to be asking it? Or do we strike others with words, or even physically, and need to examine our motives?

Jesus went to the core issue: was the blow justified? No, it wasn't. Jesus had said nothing wrong or in a wrong way. Perhaps the officer wanted to put Jesus in His place—the place that he thought a rebel belonged. But that's presuming guilt. Perhaps he struck Jesus to divert attention from Jesus' reference to the due process of seeking witnesses, thinking their testimonies might upset the plan to eliminate Jesus. "Never mind truth and justice, let's get this over with."

Under what circumstances do *we* lash out with weapons or words or in other ways? Our pattern gives a clue as to why we do it. We can learn a lot about ourselves. Are we like the officer, attempting to dominate so as to control an outcome? Do we compensate for a sense of weakness or guilt by some show of strength? Have we lost sight of God's power to accomplish His righteous goals so that we lash out in a desperate bid to control things 'for Him' (James 1:20)?

Jesus' example shows us that it's appropriate to cry foul when someone is acting unjustly. Jesus does not teach us to be doormats for people to wipe their dirty feet on. Jesus names sin gently and without condemnation because people are more likely to change under gentle conviction than the harsh, damning kind. He calls sin out once or twice and then waits for a response, rather than nagging. He leads people down the narrow path of change—if they choose it. Jesus wasn't demanding His own rights from His interrogators; rather He was calling them to deal justly. Let's be like Him to others. And let's recognize His goal when He questions us.

A Bad Question

(Context: Luke 23:8-12.)

There's a saying that there is no such thing as a bad question—but that's not entirely true. Take King Herod, for example.

> *Herod was overjoyed when he saw Jesus; for he had wanted to see Him for a long time, because he had been hearing about Him and was hoping to see some sign performed by Him. And he questioned Him at some length; but He offered him no answer at all.* (Luke 23:8-9)

The pattern was similar with other interrogators and mockers during Jesus' trial. Although Jesus gave brief answers to a few questions, He remained silent when the high priest and Pilate wanted Him to respond to false accusations (Matt. 26:59-63; 27:12-14; Mark 14:60-61; 15:3-5). In the final stages of Pilate's questioning, Jesus would not even say where He came from (John 19:9). The mocking demand for a prophetic party trick was ignored (Luke 22:63-65).

It must have been a particularly frustrating meeting for Herod. He had finally met Jesus, but the legend did no signs and would not answer a single question. Perhaps Herod was still trying to get to the bottom of his earlier puzzlement: "I myself had John beheaded; but who is this man about whom I hear such things?" (Luke 9:9) Understanding Herod's motive may help us understand why Jesus stayed silent. We can only speculate, of course, but perhaps Herod was afraid like his father, Herod the Great. Dad had ruthlessly killed all the Bethlehem boys in Jesus' age group to avoid a potential threat to his throne (Matt. 2:16). The son, Herod Antipas, heard of Jesus, the popular miracle-worker, and his superstitions suggested the worst. If John the Baptist had returned to life (Matt. 14:1-2), perhaps there would be no stopping him and his fans. Even some Pharisees once warned Jesus that Herod wanted Him dead (Luke 13:31). At best, Herod's intrigue may have amounted to idle curiosity. What better than a private magic show to alleviate royal boredom?

Surveying the pattern of Jesus' questions, and His responses to other people's questions, helps us understand why Jesus ignored Herod and others. Most of the 105 questions asked of Jesus came from disciples (38%), religious leaders (23%), and various groups of Jews or crowds (17%). The disciples asked Him questions for information and direction (22%), or to learn (50%). Most of the religious leaders' questions (64%), and of the Jews' questions (67%), had negative intent—cynicism, accusation, or attempts to trap Him. 76% of Jesus' 165 questions aimed to challenge or change people's thinking about God and His kingdom and He asked 56% of those of His followers.

Jesus responded to most questions but prioritized keen students. His disciples once asked why He spoke to the multitude in parables. Jesus explained, "To you it has been granted to know the mysteries of the kingdom of heaven, but to them it has not been granted." (Matt. 13:9-11) It boiled down to who had an open path from their physical ears to a heart receptive to God's truth. As Jesus often said, "He who has ears, let him hear."

That's something for us to think about, especially if we sense a long silence from God. Do our questions come from faith or cynicism? Are we hoping for a particular answer, or are we seeking His answer and ready to act on it? There's never a bad question—if we are genuinely seeking truth.

UPGRADE

(Context: John 20:1-18. Parallels: Matt. 28:1-10; Mark 16:1-11; Luke 24:1-12.)

Mary was standing outside the tomb, weeping; so as she wept, she stooped to look into the tomb; and she saw two angels in white sitting, one at the head and one at the feet, where the body of Jesus had been lying. And they said to her, "Woman, why are you weeping?" She said to them, "Because they have taken away my Lord, and I do not know where they have put Him." When she had said this, she turned around and saw Jesus standing there, and yet she did not know that it was Jesus. Jesus said to her, "Woman, why are you weeping? Whom are you seeking?" (John 20:11-15)

They seem like stupid questions; to us, they have obvious answers. But angels and Jesus are far from stupid. When one gets asked the same question twice, perhaps it's time to wonder if there's another answer.

One obvious answer was that Mary sought Jesus. He was the one who had dismissed her seven demon guards (Luke 8:2) and showed her what true freedom was. He was a man whose love was deep and pure, telling her truth in a way that brought out her best, a friend closer than a brother, but without the confusion of romance, and untainted by selfish lusts. She knew; she had traveled with Him since her jail break. He was her hero in other ways too. So many people had received health and deliverance. Fierce storms, fig trees, and fish obeyed Him. What a star He had become to people because of His wise and witty words! Sadly, it was because of those words and His star quality that everything had come crashing down on Thursday and Friday. That morning she was looking for the body of her beloved hero.

Her hero was limited though. He'd said and done amazing things, but they went no further than sight, sound, or gossip would carry them. How long had it been now? Perhaps three years. Ten percent of a life that was bound to end anyway, someday. In all that time, He had done nothing to tackle the burdens imposed by occupying Romans with their taxes and harsh law enforcement. He'd turned down opportunities that would surely have led to a royal title. He'd died; hope had died. That's why she was weeping.

That's why she didn't recognize Him. Her tears blurred His face; her sobs muffled His voice. Expectation blinded and deafened her.

We know the end of the story—and we cheer. But don't we face the same challenge as the Samaritan woman, and people like Mary, who saw Jesus alive again? It's hard to exchange our existing ideas of who He is for a fuller, more accurate version—an upgrade. Mary had to bury her mental image of a dead hero in order to receive a resurrected Lord.

She's an important example to us of how that exchange becomes possible. It would have been so easy for her to give up after she had seen the opened tomb. Alert Peter and John to the problem (John 20:1-2), go home, and write some memories in a journal. She didn't. She went back with the men and hung around—staring the evidence of death in the face, begging for the body. That brave behavior positioned her to meet Jesus. Not the Jesus she had believed in, but the Risen One. There's always more to experience with Him, and more to learn about resurrection life. Are you seeking the upgrade?

RESURRECTION
or RESUSCITATION?

(Context: Mark 14:32-42. Parallels: Matt. 26:36-46; Luke 22:39-46.)

I guess that most of us, when we talk about resurrection life, are stuck on resuscitation. Let's face it; we tend to love our lives, with their relationships, dreams, hopes, possessions, health, and so many other facets that give them quality. When part of us dies we want it back—scrubbed from malware, with a free subscription to the newest version. We have little or no concept of anything radically different. Resuscitation-plus will do just fine.

When Jesus claimed to be the resurrection and the life, He had more in mind (John 11:25-26). Other people had returned to life: Jairus' daughter, two women's sons, Lazarus, Dorcas, and a body thrown into Elisha's tomb all came back. But they died a second, natural death. Jesus' resurrection was different.[18]

[The two disciples'] *eyes were opened and they recognized Him; and He vanished from their sight. They said to one another, "Were not our hearts burning within us when He was speaking to us on the road, while He was explaining the Scriptures to us?"* (Luke 24:31-32)

When the doors were shut where the disciples were together due to fear of the Jews, Jesus came and stood in their midst, and said to them, "Peace be to you." And when He had said this, He showed them both His hands and His side. The disciples then rejoiced when they saw the Lord. (John 20:19-20)

---

18. Mark 5:42; Luke 7:14-15; John 11:43-44; Acts 9:40; 2 Kings 4:35; 13:21.

While they still could not believe it because of their joy and astonishment, He said to them, "Have you anything here to eat?" They served Him a piece of broiled fish; and He took it and ate it in front of them. (Luke 24:41-43)

Jesus' resurrection body spanned two dimensions. On one hand, He had scars and could participate in normal life activities like walking, talking, and eating fish. On the other hand, He could materialize in a room with closed doors and disappear from a dining table before the main course was served, let alone dessert. His presence made hearts glow.

God doesn't offer resuscitation; He gives resurrection life. In Him we become new creations. He's not withholding it until we die; we can start now. But our ordinary lives can get in the way. We should hold familiar things loosely, but we cling to our lives, don't we? Why are we so careful to defend what we have? Why expend our limited strength to guard what we fear losing? It's because the present and past are clear, while the future is uncertain. For us to receive resurrection life requires faith and a careful assessment of its immense value. Unless something is given life by God, it is not worth fighting for. Releasing each facet of this lesser life to God frees us from its potential power as an idol and makes room for His resurrection life to grow in its place.

REBOOTING
the RECRUITS

(Context: John 21:1-14.)

Actions speak louder than words. Jesus used action to reveal Himself to several disciples after His resurrection. Two travelers to Emmaus recognized Him only as He broke bread with them.[19] Thomas surrendered when he saw the open wounds in His risen body.[20]

More happened on a fishing trip in Galilee. Six disciples, including James and John, followed Peter's suggestion to go night-fishing. By dawn they had caught nothing. Tired and frustrated, they were packing up when a man on the shore yelled to them:

"Children, you do not have any fish to eat, do you?" They answered Him, "No." And He said to them, "Cast the net on the right-hand side of the boat, and you will find the fish." So they cast it, and then they were not able to haul it in because of the great quantity of fish. Therefore that disciple whom Jesus loved said to Peter, "It is the Lord!" So when Simon Peter heard that it was the Lord, he put on his outer garment (for he was stripped for work), and threw himself into the sea. (John 21:5-7)

While Peter sloshed ashore, the other six strained to tow the bursting net; it was too heavy to lift into the boat. Peter then hauled it onto the beach

---

19. Luke 24:30-31.
20. John 20:26-29.

and they began counting—just for the record. One hundred and fifty-three. High-fives all around. They had not seen a catch like this for a long time.

But it was not the first time. Peter, James, and John remembered so well that time a few years earlier when Jesus performed a similar miracle. That time, they had managed to get the bulging net into a couple of boats without sinking them. That time made such an impression on them that they left everything and pursued Jesus to learn to fish for men. Here they were, about three years later, eating breakfast with this awesome man, Jesus. His knowledge and abilities surpassed normal human capacities and He had just returned to life after an excruciating death.

Not only was the risen Jesus revealing Himself again to His disciples, He was also rebooting the call on their lives. Hardly a word was spoken. His actions said everything. "Remember."

"Remember who I am.
Remember what I am able to do.
Remember what I called you to.
Remember all that you have seen and done with me since you started to follow.
Remember the words that I spoke that have come to pass.
Remember the promises I gave you about the future."

Sometimes God takes us into circumstances that seem like spiritual déjà-vu; in fact, they are a reminder of what He has said and done in the past. They serve as confirmation of His commitment to us and as an assurance that He has forgiven us. Most of all, they gently thrust us back to obeying the call on our lives with new confidence.

As soon as breakfast was over, Jesus called out Peter's love for Him and gave him another assignment beyond fishing for men, "Tend my sheep." (John 21:15-17)

FOLLOW ME

(Context: John 21:15-23.)

For disciples, there's no such thing as arriving. If an individual or group ever thinks they are close to the stable, mature, well-functioning ideal that they have longed for and worked toward they are probably fossilizing. Jesus keeps moving; that's why we are called to follow—beyond failures, through responsibilities and sacrifices, ignoring distractions.

Jesus' three-part conversation with Peter (John 21:15-17) was the subtle giving of a second chance. A few days earlier, Peter had bragged about his undying loyalty to Jesus. That had ended in a cowardly denial of any association with Him. Memories of failure can act like an epitaph or obituary pronouncing the death and burial of good intentions. Jesus' questions probed like a physician's scope showing Peter that his love still lived and needed rehabilitation. Hence the call to shepherding.

A good under-shepherd cares for sheep on behalf of the chief shepherd. The love that Jesus calls us to is evident in an obedience that carries no guarantee of personal gain, and one that often involves risk and sacrifice. Are we willing to follow Jesus on those terms?

Jesus' second challenge was more direct and had implied questions (John 21:18-19). Will you, Peter, follow me even when it means surrendering your own freedom? Will you trust that I am guiding your path when it seems like your enemies have prevailed? Will you stay loyal enough to go through the door of death against every ounce of your instinct? If we understand early on in our walk with the Lord that there will be increasingly tough choices to make between the path that Jesus is beckoning us to take and gentler alternatives, then we will be better prepared to stay on His heels.

Peter did what so many of us do to avoid searching questions, he let a "squirrel" distract him. Seeing John following them, Peter asked, *"Lord, and what about this man?" Jesus said to him, "If I want him to remain until I come, what is that to you? You follow Me!"* (John 21:21-23)

It's so easy to lose focus on Jesus if we sense that others have things easier or better. We want life to be fair. If their path looks gentler, why can't we walk it? The envious question is irrelevant. We will falter if we compare ourselves with others instead of attending to Jesus' next move.

Jesus' response was wise. He let the cause of envy linger as a possibility (like the squirrel sitting on a branch shaking its tail at a salivating dog) while He challenged Peter to his own obedience. It would have been easy to dismiss the possibility of super-longevity for John in order to reassure Peter of fairness, but obedience is tested better in the presence of trials.

The idea of favoritism irks us. How could Jesus single out a beloved disciple? But did He? Wasn't it perhaps that John, the author, identified himself in that way simply because Jesus made Him feel especially loved? And was it Jesus who loved John differently, or was it John's understanding of Jesus, and his faith in Him, that resulted in a deeper bond between them—we call it connection? Relationships are a two-way street; love flows best when the lanes are wide and smooth in both directions.

Ironically, Jesus interacted more with Peter than with John. Yet John was secure in the depth of his relationship with Jesus. That depth came from trust and understanding, not extra attention. Attention can be skin deep; shared heartbeats are profound.

MAKING ISRAEL GREAT AGAIN

(Context: Acts 1:1-8)

Straddling two positions is awkward—spiritually too. Jesus' followers live in two kingdoms—the kingdom of God and that of the world. The world is inescapably close and screams; God's kingdom comes, slow and gentle, like sprouting corn. Its fullness lies in a misty future. It's easy to become confused.

Six weeks after Jesus rose from the dead, His disciples still put their weight on the wrong foot. They asked:

"Lord, is it at this time that You are restoring the kingdom to Israel?" But He said to them, "It is not for you to know periods of time or appointed times which the Father has set by His own authority; but you will receive power when the Holy Spirit has come upon you; and you will be My witnesses." (Acts 1:6-8)

Their question reveals what excited them and how limited their understanding of God's plan still was. The resurrection had proved that Jesus was Lord and Messiah (Acts 2:36; Rom. 1:4). But, like other Jews, they expected the Messiah to make Israel great again. "Out with the Romans." "Down with corrupt leaders and traitorous tax-gatherers. (Not you, Matthew. You're Okay.)" "Jesus is King." As loyal Jewish disciples, those were their heart cries.

Eventually, Jesus disses everyone's illusions and bursts everyone's bubbles. Not this time. Jesus hardly acknowledged their question. No correction. No explanation. No need! Things were moving right along: Ascension, Pentecost ten days later, and then a divinely orchestrated outpouring of the Spirit on (cough) a Roman stronghold. That outpouring finally opened Peter's eyes to God's plan for a pan-ethnic kingdom extending beyond tiny Israel's borders.

Whatever excites us and fills our expectations becomes a source of anxiety when it is threatened. That's why Peter had grabbed a sword to protect his king (John 18:10). And it's why we get riled about so much on earth: politics, economics, climate change, bad laws, and broken laws. You've read the petitions and placards. As citizens of two kingdoms, only clarity about the kingdom of God will free us from anxiety and swordplay. Jesus was clear. In one of His rare answers to Pilate, He assured the governor that His kingdom was not of this world and did not require a fight (John 18:36).

Like all the seed-like words of Jesus, this truth about the kingdom will fall on various heart surfaces. Some will be hard, some distracted, but others will take encouragement and grow more fruitful as Jesus' witnesses. So, let's prepare our hearts. Then, to paraphrase one of Jesus' favorite endings, if we have spiritual ears, let's use them (Matt. 13:9).

MISGUIDED

(Context: Acts 9:1-22; 26:12-18.)

As [Saul] was traveling, it happened that he was approaching Damascus, and suddenly a light from heaven flashed around him; and he fell to the ground and heard a voice saying to him, "Saul, Saul, why are you persecuting me?" And he said, "Who are you, Lord?" (Acts 9:3-5)

We have to admit that Saul[21] was not knowingly persecuting Jesus. Until the blinding flash, Saul would have explained his passionate hunt for members of 'the Way' as a defense of Judaism against blasphemy. That was the charge against Stephen and the evidence sought against others (Acts 6:11; 26:11). To Saul, Jesus was nothing more than a blasphemous nuisance, eradicated to prevent his influence spreading and destabilizing Judea. Jesus had been presented as a resurrected martyr by misguided followers who had somehow stolen his body. Saul was driven to silence those crazed followers before they did more damage.

The voice changed things. Instantly, Jesus went from being a dead rebel to a living Lord. Suddenly, everything Saul had studied intensely as a Pharisee melted down and had to be recast in a new mould. Orthodox interpretations

---

21. Later, Saul became better known as Paul (Acts 13:9).

of Scriptures about the Messiah, the Law, and the nature of God's people, the Jews, were all called into question as the voice identified itself, "I am Jesus whom you are persecuting." In a flash, the Jewish religious authorities were exposed as the misguided ones. If they had been wrong about Jesus, didn't that make them the blasphemers?

Saul's change was easier than most people's because His Scripture-steeped culture provided a stepping stone to faith in Jesus. Once Saul knew that Jesus was alive and communicating with him, he began to reinterpret the Old Testament and saw how it pointed to Jesus. The voice and the light were part of God's plan to prepare Saul as a chosen instrument to explain Jesus to the world (Acts 9:15; 26:16-18).

Jewish religious leaders persecuted Jesus because they were convinced that their understanding of a relationship with God was correct. After all, their views were based on Scripture and had been taught by respected teachers for centuries. Their authority had been handed down over generations; it was so baked into the Jewish culture that the mob obediently shouted, "Crucify," with hardly a thought.

Persecution is a strong word. But even if we stop short of doing that, at those times when we unknowingly fight against or reject Jesus' ways, we need to ask ourselves, "Why?" What is baked into our lives along with justifications for ignoring or resisting Jesus? Often it boils down to not knowing or trusting His care, His power, and that His plans for us are best. What do we hold as the defining distinctions of our particular creed and practices? Did Jesus hold the same ones, or do ours come from political ideologies or extra-biblical traditions? Such things are deeply rooted and can be hard to trace through self-examination. The risen Jesus who questioned Saul still uses questions to draw us out of our old ways and deeper into His own. If we are to avoid misguidedly clashing with Jesus, we must nurture a humility that welcomes His light and His voice.

If you enjoyed this book, please spread the word so that other people can be blessed. Honest reader reviews and recommendations help authors. Posting reviews on sites like Amazon.com is quite simple. You can paste the same review at other online booksellers and your Social Media pages and in emails. People can buy my books at Amazon.com or BibleMaturity.com or NamesForGod.net.

Find the book on the bookseller's site. Scroll down until you find reviews and a button which allows you to post your own review. Then paste in or write your review. Leave a star rating too.

Sites that have a place for reviews (*these require a free account):

Amazon.com	*Goodreads.com	Walmart.com	*LibraryThing.com
Powells.com	BooksAMillion.com	BarnesandNoble.com	Books.google.com	ChristianBook.com
Kobo.com			

For news about other publications:

- "Follow" me as an author on Amazon
- Sign up for a quarterly newsletter by scrolling down the sidebar at www.NamesForGod.net
- Sign up to receive devotionals posted on my blog site www.BibleMaturity.com

ABOUT
the AUTHOR

John Avery is the author of *The Name Quest: Explore the Names of God to Grow in Faith and Get to Know Him Better* (Morgan James Publishing, 2015). *The Name Quest* won the 2016 Oregon Christian Writers' Cascade Award for nonfiction.

John is a trained teacher with over thirty years' experience as a Bible teaching pastor, small group leader, and missionary. He has lived in England, Israel, Africa, and the Caribbean, ministering with Youth With A Mission (YWAM), international student ministry, and local churches. He and his wife, Janet, now make their home in Oregon. John likes to hike, snowshoe, and cross-country ski. John writes short, thought-provoking Bible devotionals at *www.BibleMaturity.com* many of which are being compiled in book form. He maintains a comprehensive resource for all the names of God at *www.NamesForGod.net*.

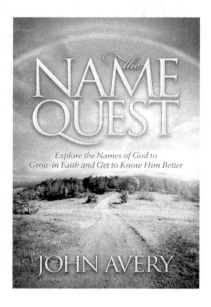

**Watch for future compilations
in the Sparks Series on topics like:**

The Kingdom of God

Our Identity as Children of God

Talking to God

Faith in God

The Spirit of God

Following the Voice of God

Revival from God

Prophets of God

Names of God

Followers of Jesus

Kings of Israel
(David, Saul, and others)

Fathers of Faith
(Abraham, Jacob, and Moses)

Various other in-depth devotionals are at
www.BibleMaturity.com

THE SPARKS SERIES

CPSIA information can be obtained
at www.ICGtesting.com
Printed in the USA
JSHW020238280922
31078JS00004B/19